HA

Verbs

Compiled by
LEXUS
with
Jane Goldie

HARRAP
EDINBURGH
PARIS NEW YORK

First published in Great Britain 1989
by HARRAP BOOKS Ltd
43–45 Annandale Street
Edinburgh EH7 4AZ

ISBN 0 245-54745-2

Reprinted 1990, 1993

Printed in England by Clays Ltd, St Ives plc

INTRODUCTION

The main body of this book is a dictionary of English phrasal verbs, those vital and flexible elements of the English language. Over 1,000 of these are presented, analysed and put into contexts to show typical, modern, everyday usage. But the book is more than this. It is a survey of the structure of English verbs and of their usage. It ranges from auxiliaries to tense forms, from modals to gerunds. But these technical terms need present no problem, since full explanations have always been provided. And in addition to this, there is a glossary of relevant grammatical terminology on pages 7-10. Above all, this book has made full use of example sentences to show English verbs and verbal constructions as they are actually used.

CONTENTS

1 GLOSSARY OF GRAMMATICAL TERMS

ACTIVE The active form of a verb is the basic form as in *I remember him*. It is normally opposed to the passive form of the verb as in *he will be remembered*.

AUXILIARY Auxiliary verbs are used to form compound tenses of other verbs, eg ***have*** in ***I have*** *seen* or ***will*** in *she* ***will*** *go*. The main auxiliary verbs are ***be***, ***do*** and ***have***.

BASE See INFINITIVE.

CLAUSE A clause is a group of words which contains at least a subject and a verb: *he left* is a clause. Sentences can be made up of several clauses: *he left/ when he realized/ what was going to happen*.

COLLOQUIAL Colloquial language is the sort of language that can be used in everyday informal conversation but is avoided in formal writing such as legal contracts etc.

COMPOUND Compound tenses are verb tenses consisting of more than one element. They are formed by the **auxiliary** verb and the **present** or **past participle**: *I was only asking, she hadn't been expecting that, they have already gone*.

CONDITIONAL This mood is used to describe what someone would do, or something that would happen if a condition were fulfilled (eg *I* ***would come*** *if I was well*; *the chair* ***would have broken*** *if he had sat on it*).

CONJUGATION The conjugation of a verb is the set of different forms taken in the particular tenses or moods of that verb.

CONTINUOUS The continuous form of a verb is formed with *to be* + **present participle**, for example, *I am thinking, he has been writing all day, will she be staying with us?* This is also called the 'progressive'.

GERUND A gerund is also called a 'verbal noun'. It has the same form as the **present participle** of a verb, ie base + **-ing**. Examples are: *skiing is fun, I'm fed up with waiting*.

IMPERATIVE A mood used for giving orders (eg *stop!*, *don't go!*) or for making suggestions (eg *let's go*).

INDICATIVE The normal form of a verb as in *I like*, *he came*, *we are trying*. It is opposed to the subjunctive, conditional and imperative.

INFINITIVE The infinitive is the form of the verb as found in dictionaries. Thus *(to) eat*, *(to) finish*, *(to) take* are infinitives.

INTERROGATIVE Interrogative words are used to ask questions, for example *who?, why?*. The interrogative form of a sentence is the question form, for example *does he know?, do I have to?, can they wait a bit?*

MODALS The modal auxiliaries are the words *can/could, may/might, must/had to, shall/should, will/would*. Also *ought to, used to, dare* and *need*. One of their main features is that question and negative forms are constructed without the use of the auxiliary *do*.

MOOD The name given to the four main areas within which a verb can be used. See INDICATIVE, SUBJUNCTIVE, CONDITIONAL, IMPERATIVE.

OBJECT There are two types of object: direct and indirect. The sentence *I sent Roger a fax* has two objects. *A fax* is the direct object (what I sent); *Roger* is the indirect object (to whom it was sent). In the sentence *I phoned Roger to check*, however, *Roger* is the direct object.

PASSIVE A verb is used in the passive when the subject of the verb does not perform the action but is subjected to it. In English, the passive is formed with a part of the verb *to be* and the past participle of the verb, eg *he was rewarded*.

PAST PARTICIPLE The past participle of a verb is the form which is used after *to have*, eg *I have* ***eaten***, *I have* ***said***, *you have* ***tried***, *it has been* ***rained*** *on*.

PERSON In any tense, there are three persons in the singular (1st: *I* . . ., 2nd: *you* . . ., 3rd: *he/she* . . .), and three in the plural (1st: *we* . . ., 2nd: *you* . . ., 3rd: *they* . . .).

PHRASAL VERB A phrasal verb is a verb of the type *go in for* or *run up*. They usually have a meaning which is more than the sum of their parts, for example *he goes in for skiing in a big way* (contrast: *he goes in for a medical next week*), *he ran up an* *enormous bill* (contrast: *he ran up the road*).

PRESENT PARTICIPLE The present participle is the verb form which ends in *-ing*.

PRONOUNS A pronoun is a word which stands for a noun. There are many different types. Personal pronouns are *I, me, you, he, him, she, her, we, us, they, them*. Demonstrative pronouns are *this, that, these, those*.

REFLEXIVE Reflexive verbs 'reflect' the action back onto the subject (eg *I dressed myself*).

SUBJECT The subject of a verb is the noun or pronoun which performs the action. In the sentences *the train left early* and *she bought a record*, *the train* and *she* are the subjects.

SUBJUNCTIVE The subjunctive is a verb form which is not often used in English (eg *if I were you, God save the Queen, be they friend or foe*).

SUBORDINATE CLAUSE A group of words with a subject and a verb which is dependent on another clause. For example, in *he said he would leave*, *he would leave* is the subordinate clause dependent on *he said*.

TENSE Verbs are used in tenses, which indicate when an action takes place, eg in the present, the past, the future.

VOICE The two voices of a verb are its active and passive forms.

2 VERB FORMS: KEY CONCEPTS

Key concepts are:

infinitive or base
present participle
past participle

i) The **infinitive** or **base** is the form of the verb as given in the headword in the phrasal verb dictionary of this book or in the index. This form can be used with or without the word **to**. **Watch** is in the infinitive in:

do you want to watch?

I can't watch

ii) The **present participle** is a form of the verb ending in **-ing**:

is anyone watching?

they were watching us

Note that, as in the last example, this present participle is used to form tenses other than present tenses.

For the various spelling rules affecting present participles see section 5.

iii) There are two basic types of **past participle** of a verb. For regular verbs the past participle is identical with the simple past tense, ie base + **-(e)d**:

watch – watched

dance – danced

For details of the spelling rules affecting past participles see section 5.

Past participles of irregular verbs are given in the list on p 22. Examples are:

go – went

teach – taught

stand – stood

3 AUXILIARIES

The verbs **be**, **do** and **have** are known as primary auxiliaries. As well as functioning as verbs in their own right (**I am over here; do something quick!; have another**) they are used to form tenses:

what ARE you doing?

what DO you do?

what HAVE you done?

The forms of these auxiliaries in the present and past tense are:

be
present tense

	singular	*plural*
1st	**I am**	**we are**
2nd	**you are**	**you are**
3rd	**he/she/it is**	**they are**

past tense

	singular	*plural*
1st	**I was**	**we were**
2nd	**you were**	**you were**
3rd	**he/she/it was**	**they were**

do
present tense

	singular	*plural*
1st	**I do**	**we do**
2nd	**you do**	**you do**
3rd	**he/she/it does**	**they do**

past tense

	singular	*plural*
1st	**I did**	**we did**
2nd	**you did**	**you did**
3rd	**he/she/it did**	**they did**

have
present tense

	singular	*plural*
1st	**I have**	**we have**
2nd	**you have**	**you have**
3rd	**he/she/it has**	**they have**

past tense

	singular	*plural*
1st	**I had**	**we had**
2nd	**you had**	**you had**
3rd	**he/she/it had**	**they had**

4 TENSES

In English the majority of verbs have the same endings for all persons in a tense, for example:

I/you/he/she/it/we/they went

The main exception is the third person singular of the present tense. This ends is **-s** or **-es** (see spelling patterns in section 5), for example:

	singular	*plural*
1st	**I watch**	**we watch**
2nd	**you watch**	**you watch**
3rd	**he/she/it watches**	**they watch**

Verb tenses are formed as follows (for usage see sections 16 – 18, for the Passive see section 6):

infinitive simple	**(to) watch**
infinitive continuous	**(to) be watching** (**be** + present participle)
infinitive perfect(ive)	**(to) have watched** (**have** + past participle)
infinitive perfect(ive) continuous	**(to) have been watching**
present simple	**(I/you/he** etc) **watch(es)**
present continuous	**am/are/is watching**
*future simple**	**will watch**
*future continuous**	**will be watching**
past simple	**watched**
past continuous	**was/were watching**

present perfect(ive)	**have/has watched**
present perfect(ive) continuous	**have/has been watching**
past perfect(ive)	**had watched**
past perfect(ive) continuous	**had been watching**
future perfect	**will have watched**
future perfect continuous	**will have been watching**
present conditional	**would watch**
present conditional continuous	**would be watching**
past conditional	**would have watched**
past conditional continuous	**would have been watching**

The 'continuous' is sometimes called the 'progressive'; and some (older) grammars refer to the 'present perfect(ive)' as the 'perfect', and to the 'past perfect' as the 'pluperfect'.

* In modern theory the 'future' is not regarded as a separate tense in English.

5 VERB PATTERNS

This section gives a breakdown of verbs into various types or patterns according to the spelling variations that occur. The verbs in the index of this book are coded with a pattern reference.

P1

	add
'he/she/it' in present	**-s**
present participle	**-ing**
past participle	**-ed**

For example:

look: looks – looking – looked

P2

	add
'he/she/it' in present	**-es**
present participle	**-ing**
past participle	**-ed**

For example:

watch: watches – watching – watched

NOTE: **-es** is added to verbs ending in **-s**, **-x**, **-z**, **-ch** and **-sh**.

P3

	add
'he/she/it' in present	**-s**
present participle	**-ing**
past participle	**-d**

For example:

agree: agrees – agreeing – agreed

P4

	drop	*add*
'he/she/it' in present		**-s**
present participle	final **-e**	**-ing**
past participle		**-d**

For example:

hate: hates – hating – hated

P5

	add	*changes*
'he/she/it' in present	**-s**	
present participle	**-ing**	double final consonant
past participle	**-ed**	double final consonant

For example:

grab: grabs – grabbing – grabbed

occur: occurs – occurring – occurred

NOTE: this doubling occurs after a short stressed vowel as in the above examples. But not in for example:

keep: keeps – keeping

where the vowel is long. Or in:

vomit: vomits – vomiting – vomited

where the vowel is not stressed.

In BRITISH English this doubling occurs even after an unstressed final vowel as in:

travel: travels – travelling – travelled

kidnap: kidnaps – kidnapping – kidnapped

But AMERICAN spelling keeps the single consonant:

kidnap – kidnaping – kidnaped

travel – traveling – traveled

(Am) in the index indicates verbs that follow this American pattern.

P6

	change	*add*
'he/she/it' in present	final **y** to **ies**	
present participle		**-ing**
past participle	final **y** to **ied**	

For example:

accompany: accompanies – accompanying – accompanied

cry: cries – crying – cried

P7

	change	*add*
'he/she/it' in present		**-s**
present participle	final **ie** to **y**	**-ing**
past participle		**-d**

For example:

die: dies – dying – died

P8

	change	*add*
'he/she/it' in present		**-s**
present participle	final **c** to **ck**	**-ing**
past participle	final **c** to **ck**	**-ed**

For example:

picnic: picnics – picknicking – picknicked

P9

This code is used when the past participle is irregular (see p 22). It can occur in combination with other codes, for example:

choose: chooses – choosing – chosen

In these cases the coding is, for example, P4 P9. The P9 obviously overrides the pattern of P4 as regards the past participle.

P10

	add
'he/she/it' in present	**-ses**
present participle	**-sing**
past participle	**-sed**

A rare form:

non-plus: non-plusses – non-plussing – non-plussed

6 THE PASSIVE

In the sentence:

I follow

the verb 'follow is 'active' and the subject 'I' performs the action of following. But in the sentence:

I am followed

the verb 'am followed' is 'passive' and the subject 'I' is exposed to the action of being followed.

i) The passive is formed with the verb **be** + the past participle. For example, the verb **hide**:

infinitive simple	**(to) be hidden**
infinitive perfect(ive)	**(to) have been hidden**
infinitive continuous	**(to) be being hidden**
present simple	**am/are/is hidden**
present continuous	**am/are/is being hidden**
future simple	**will be hidden**
future continuous	**will be being hidden**
past simple	**was/were hidden**
past continuous	**was/were being hidden**
present perfect(ive)	**have/has been hidden**
present perfect(ive) continuous	**have/has been being hidden**
past perfect(ive)	**had been hidden**
past perfect(ive) continuous	**had been being hidden**
future perfect	**will have been hidden**

present conditional	**would be hidden**
present conditional continuous	**would be being hidden**
past conditional	**would have been hidden**
past conditional continuous	**would have been being hidden**

Examples:

it was hidden under some old papers

it had deliberately been hidden by his assistant

it was thought to have been hidden by the Ancient Celts

he objected to this information being hidden away at the bottom of the form

if he were a suspect, he would be being asked a lot of questions by now

if he had made any comment it would almost certainly have been ignored

ii) Note that the active sentence:

they sent him the wrong letter

can be expressed in the passive in either of two ways:

the wrong letter was sent to him

he was sent the wrong letter

iii) Intransitive verbs can often be used with a passive sense:

it opens at the front

the sentence reads better like this

this material won't wash very well

7 IRREGULAR VERBS

American forms have been indicated by *. Unusual, archaic or literary forms are given in brackets.

infinitive	*past simple*	*past participle*
abide	**(abode)** [1]	**abided**
arise	**arose**	**arisen**
awake	**awoke, awaked**	**awoken, (awaked)**
bear	**bore**	**borne** [2]
beat	**beat**	**beaten** [3]
become	**became**	**become**
befall	**befell**	**befallen**
beget	**begot**	**begotten**
begin	**began**	**begun**
behold	**beheld**	**beheld**
bend	**bent**	**bent** [4]
bereave	**bereaved**	**bereft** [5]
beseech	**besought**	**besought**
bestride	**bestrode**	**bestridden**
bet	**bet, betted**	**bet, betted**
bid (*offer*)	**bid**	**bid**
bid (*command*)	**bade**	**bidden**
bind	**bound**	**bound**
bite	**bit**	**bitten**
bleed	**bled**	**bled**
blow	**blew**	**blown**
break	**broke**	**broken** [6]
breed	**bred**	**bred**
bring	**brought**	**brought**
broadcast	**broadcast**	**broadcast**
build	**built**	**built**
burn	**burnt, burned**	**burnt, burned**
burst	**burst**	**burst**
buy	**bought**	**bought**
cast	**cast**	**cast**
catch	**caught**	**caught**
chide	**chid, chided**	**chid, (chidden), chided**

choose	**chose**	**chosen**
cleave (*cut*)	**clove, cleft,**	**cloven, cleft** [7]
cleave (*adhere*)	**cleaved, (clave)**	**cleaved**
cling	**clung**	**clung**
clothe	**clothed, (clad)**	**clothed, (clad)**
come	**came**	**come**
cost	**cost**	**cost**
creep	**crept**	**crept**
crow	**crowed, (crew)**	**crowed**
cut	**cut**	**cut**
dare	**dared, (durst)**	**dared, (durst)**
deal	**dealt**	**dealt**
dig	**dug**	**dug**
dive	**dived, dove***	**dived**
draw	**drew**	**drawn**
dream	**dreamt, dreamed**	**dreamt, dreamed**
drink	**drank**	**drunk** [8]
drive	**drove**	**driven**
dwell	**dwelt, dwelled**	**dwelt, dwelled**
eat	**ate**	**eaten**
fall	**fell**	**fallen**
feed	**fed**	**fed**
feel	**felt**	**felt**
fight	**fought**	**fought**
find	**found**	**found**
fit	**fit*, fitted**	**fit*, fitted**
flee	**fled**	**fled**
fling	**flung**	**flung**
fly	**flew**	**flown**
forbear	**forbore**	**forborne**
forbid	**forbad(e)**	**forbidden**
forget	**forgot**	**forgotten**
forgive	**forgave**	**forgiven**
forsake	**forsook**	**forsaken**
freeze	**froze**	**frozen**
get	**got**	**got, gotten*** [9]
gild	**gilt, gilded**	**gilt, gilded** [10]
gird	**girt, girded**	**girt, girded** [10]
give	**gave**	**given**
go	**went**	**gone**

grind	ground	ground
grow	grew	grown
hang	hung, hanged [11]	hung, hanged [11]
hear	heard	heard
heave	hove, heaved [12]	hove, heaved [12]
hew	hewed	hewn, hewed
hide	hid	hidden
hit	hit	hit
hold	held	held
hurt	hurt	hurt
keep	kept	kept
kneel	knelt, kneeled	knelt, kneeled
knit	knit, knitted [13]	knit, knitted [13]
know	knew	known
lay	laid	laid
lead	led	led
lean	leant, leaned	leant, leaned
leap	leapt, leaped	leapt, leaped
learn	learnt, learned	learnt, learned
leave	left	left
lend	lent	lent
let	let	let
lie	lay	lain
light	lit, lighted	lit, lighted [14]
lose	lost	lost
make	made	made
mean	meant	meant
meet	met	met
melt	melted	melted, molten [15]
mow	mowed	mown, mowed
pay	paid	paid
plead	pled*, pleaded	pled*, pleaded [16]
put	put	put
quit	quit, (quitted)	quit, (quitted) [17]
read	read	read
rend	rent	rent
rid	rid, (ridded)	rid
ride	rode	ridden
ring	rang	rung
rise	rose	risen

run	**ran**	**run**
saw	**sawed**	**sawn, sawed**
say	**said**	**said**
see	**saw**	**seen**
seek	**sought**	**sought**
sell	**sold**	**sold**
send	**sent**	**sent**
set	**set**	**set**
sew	**sewed**	**sewn, sewed**
shake	**shook**	**shaken**
shear	**sheared**	**shorn, sheared** [18]
shed	**shed**	**shed**
shine	**shone**	**shone** [19]
shoe	**shod, shoed**	**shod, shoed** [20]
shoot	**shot**	**shot**
show	**showed**	**shown, showed**
shrink	**shrank, shrunk**	**shrunk, shrunken** [21]
shut	**shut**	**shut**
sing	**sang**	**sung**
sink	**sank**	**sunk, sunken** [22]
sit	**sat**	**sat**
slay	**slew**	**slain**
sleep	**slept**	**slept**
slide	**slid**	**slid**
sling	**slung**	**slung**
slink	**slunk**	**slunk**
slit	**slit**	**slit**
smell	**smelt, smelled**	**smelt, smelled**
smite	**smote**	**smitten**
sneak	**snuck*, sneaked**	**snuck*, sneaked**
sow	**sowed**	**sown, sowed**
speak	**spoke**	**spoken**
speed	**sped, speeded**	**sped, speeded**
spell	**spelt, spelled**	**spelt, spelled**
spend	**spent**	**spent**
spill	**spilt, spilled**	**spilt, spilled**
spin	**spun**	**spun**
spit	**spat, spit***	**spat, spit***

split	**split**	**split**
spoil	**spoilt, spoiled**	**spoilt, spoiled**
spread	**spread**	**spread**
spring	**sprang**	**sprung**
stand	**stood**	**stood**
steal	**stole**	**stolen**
stick	**stuck**	**stuck**
sting	**stung**	**stung**
stink	**stank**	**stunk**
strew	**strewed**	**strewn, strewed**
stride	**strode**	**stridden**
strike	**struck**	**struck, stricken** [23]
string	**strung**	**strung**
strive	**strove**	**striven**
swear	**swore**	**sworn**
sweat	**sweat*, sweated**	**sweat*, sweated**
sweep	**swept**	**swept**
swell	**swelled**	**swollen, swelled** [24]
swim	**swam**	**swum**
swing	**swung**	**swung**
take	**took**	**taken**
teach	**taught**	**taught**
tear	**tore**	**torn**
tell	**told**	**told**
think	**thought**	**thought**
thrive	**thrived, (throve)**	**thrived, (thriven)**
throw	**threw**	**thrown**
thrust	**thrust**	**thrust**
tread	**trod**	**trodden**
understand	**understood**	**understood**
undertake	**undertook**	**undertaken**
wake	**woke, waked**	**woken, waked**
wear	**wore**	**worn**
weave	**wove** [25]	**woven** [25]
weep	**wept**	**wept**
wet	**wet*, wetted** [26]	**wet*, wetted** [26]
win	**won**	**won**
wind	**wound**	**wound**
wring	**wrung**	**wrung**
write	**wrote**	**written**

(1) Regular in the combination **abide by** 'obey': **they abided by the rules**.

(2) But **born** if in the passive = 'given birth to' or as an adjective: **he was born in France/a born gentleman.**

(3) Note the colloquial **this has me beat/you have me beat there** and **beat** in the sense of very tired: **I am (dead) beat**.

(4) Note the phrase **on one's bended knees**.

(5) But **bereaved** if it implies loss by death, as in **the bereaved received no compensation.** Compare: **he was bereft of speech**.

(6) But **broke** as an adjective = without money: **I'm broke**.

(7) **Cleft** can only be used in the sense 'to cut in two'. Note **cleft palate** and **(to be caught) in a cleft stick**, but **cloven foot/hoof**.

(8) As an adjective before a noun **drunken** 'intoxicated, given to drink' is sometimes used (**a lot of drunk(en) people**) and **must** be used before inanimate nouns (**one of his usual drunken parties**).

(9) But **have got to** also in American when it means 'must': **a man has got to do what a man has got to do**. Compare: **she has gotten into a terrible mess**.

(10) Past participle **gilt** and **girt** are particularly common as adjectives before nouns: **gilt mirrors, a flower-girt grave** (but always **gilded youth**, where **gilded** means 'rich and fortunate').

(11) Regular in the sense 'execute by hanging'.

(12) **Hove** is nautical language whence the phrase **heave into sight**: **just then Mary hove into sight**.

(13) Irregular in the sense 'join closely' (**a close-knit family**), but normally regular in the sense 'make woollen garments' and when referring to bones.

(14) When the past participle is used as an adjective before a noun, lighted is often preferred to **lit**: **a lighted match** (but: **the match is lit, she has lit a match**). In compounds **lit** is used: **well-lit streets/the streets are well-lit**. In the figurative sense (with **up**) only **lit** is used in the past tense and past participle: **her face lit up when she saw me**.

(15) Only **molten** as an adjective before nouns, and only when it means 'melted at a very high temperature', eg **molten lead** (but **melted butter**).

(16) Past tense and past participle **pled** also in Scottish and American English.

(17) In American English the regular forms do not occur, and they are becoming increasingly rare in British English.

(18) The past participle is normally **shorn** before a noun (**newly-shorn lambs**) and always in the phrase **(to be) shorn of** '(to be) deprived of': **shorn of his riches he was nothing**.

(19) But regular in the sense 'polish' (American English).

(20) Only **shod** as an adjective: **a well-shod foot.**

(21) **Shrunken** is used only as an adjective: **shrunken limbs/her face was shrunken**.

(22) Sunken is used only as an adjective: **sunken eyes/her cheeks were sunken**.

(23) **Stricken** only in the figurative sense (**a stricken family/stricken with poverty**). It is particularly common in compounds: **poverty-stricken**, **fever-stricken**, **horror-stricken** (also **horror-struck**), **terror-stricken** (also **terror-struck**), but we always say **thunderstruck** 'very surprised'.

Also American usage as in 'the remark was stricken off the record'.

(24) **Swollen** is more common than **swelled** both as a verb (**her face has swollen**) and as an adjective (**her face is swollen/a swollen face**). A **swollen head** 'a high opinion of oneself' is a **swelled head** in American English.

(25) But regular when it means 'to move in and out': **the motorbike weaved elegantly through the traffic**.

(26) But irregular also in British English in the sense 'to wet with urine': **he wet his bed again last night**.

8 CONTRACTIONS

Contracted forms are very common in everyday spoken English and in non-formal writing:

BE

I am	**I'm**
you are	**you're**
he/she/it is	**he's/she's/it's**
we/they are	**we're/they're**
I am not	**I'm not**
you are not	**you're not, you aren't**
he/she/it is not	**he's/she's/it's not, he/she/it/isn't**
we/they are not	**we/they aren't**
am I not?	**aren't I?**
are you not?	**aren't you?**
is he/she/it not?	**isn't he/she/it?**
are we/they not?	**aren't we/they?**

DO

I/you/we/they do not	**I/you/we/they don't**
he/she/it does not	**he/she/it doesn't**
do I/you/we/they not?	**don't I/you/we/they?**
does he/she/it not?	**doesn't he/she/it?**

HAVE

I have	**I've**
you/we/they have	**you've/we've/they've**
he/she/it has	**he's/she's/it's** (more usual with present perfect as in **I've seen** *etc*)
I/you/we/they have not	**I/you/we/they haven't**
he/she/it/has not	**he/she/it hasn't**

have I/you/we/they not?	**haven't I/you/we/they?**
has he/she/it not?	**hasn't he/she/it?**
I/he/she/it was not	**I/he/she/it wasn't**
you/we/they were not	**you/we/they weren't**
I *etc* **did not**	**I** *etc* **didn't**
I/you *etc* **will**	**I'll/you'll** *etc*
I/he *etc* **will not**	**I/he** *etc* **won't**
I shall	**I'll**
I shall not	**I shan't**
I/you *etc* **would***	**I'd/you'd** *etc*
I/you *etc* **would not***	**I/you** *etc* **wouldn't**
I/he *etc* **would have***	**I'd've/he'd've** *etc*
I/he *etc* **would not have***	**I/he** *etc* **wouldn't have**

* also for **should** in the first person

Of course, contractions are not only used with personal pronouns:

that'll be the day!

Mummy's just gone out

See also Modal Auxiliaries, p 42.

9 QUESTIONS

i) If no other auxiliary is in use (a part of **be** or **have** or **will**) questions are formed by using the auxiliary **do**:

do you like whisky?

how do you spell it?

doesn't she expect you home?

did you talk to him?

didn't I tell you so!

ii) If another auxiliary is in use then auxiliary and subject are inverted:

he is Welsh

is he Welsh?

they're going home tomorrow

are they going home tomorrow?

Daphne will be there too

will Daphne be there too?

I can't understand

why can't I understand?

iii) If the subject is an interrogative pronoun **do** is not used:

who made that noise?

what happened?

iv) Question-tags:

a) An affirmative clause is followed by a negative tag and vice versa:

you can see it, can't you?

you can't see it, can you?

But if the tag expresses an emphatic attitude (possessive or negative) rather than a question, then an affirmative tag follows an affirmative clause:

so you've seen a ghost, have you? (disbelief, sarcasm)

he's got married again, has he? (surprise, interest)

Note that the question tag copies the tense of the main clause:

you want to meet him, don't you?

you wanted to meet him, didn't you?

you'll want to meet him, won't you?

b) If the preceding clause has an auxiliary, that auxiliary is repeated in the tag:

he has been here before, hasn't he?

they aren't stopping, are they?

you will sign it, won't you?

c) If there is no auxiliary in the preceding clause, the tag normally has **do**:

he lives in France, doesn't he?

she left yesterday, didn't she?

d) If the tag follows an imperative the auxiliary (especially **will/would**) is used. Such tags often prevent abruptness:

leave the cat alone, will you?

take this to Mrs Brown, would you?

In such cases the negative **won't** indicates an invitation:

help yourselves to drinks, won't you?

10 NEGATIVES

i) Where there is no other auxiliary (**be**, **will** etc), **not** is used together with **do** (see also Contractions, page 30):

I like the sound of it

I do not (don't) like the sound of it

she agrees with them

she does not (doesn't) agree with them

I expected him to say that

I didn't expect him to say that

ii) If another auxiliary is in use then just **not** is used:

I will (I'll) take them with me

I will not (won't) take them with me

they are just what I'm looking for

they are not really what I'm looking for (contraction = they aren't/they're not)

iii) With infinitives and gerunds **not** is used:

to be or not to be

please try not to be so stupid

it would have been better not to have mentioned it at all

he's worried about not having enough money

See also the Imperative, p 35.

11 THE IMPERATIVE

i) For the imperative the base form or infinitive (without **to**) is used:

stop that!

well, just look at him!

somebody do something!

have another

try one of mine

ii) To make suggestions in the first person plural **let's** + base form is used:

let's leave it at that for today

let's just agree to differ

iii) Negative imperatives:

To form the negative imperative place **do not** or **don't** in front of the base form. In ordinary spoken English **don't** is far more common unless special emphasis is required:

don't listen to what he says

please don't feel you have to accept

look, I've told you before, do not put your hands on the hotplate!

With the **let's** form **not** is positioned between **let's** and the verb, or the form **don't let's** can be used:

let's not go just yet

don't let's go just yet

iv) On signs and notices the form **do not** is common:

do not feed the animals

v) To stress an imperative the auxiliary **do** can be used:

oh, do be quiet!

12 EXPRESSING CONDITIONS

The sentence:

if you don't hurry, you'll miss your train

is a conditional sentence. The condition is expressed in the subordinate clause (starting with **if**) which can be placed before or after the main clause ('you'll miss your train').

Verb forms vary according to the **time reference** and the degree of **reality** of the condition.

i) Reference to present/future time:

a) 'reality' strong:

Verb in the **if**-clause in the present tense or the present perfect; main clause has **will** + infinitive: (sometimes **shall** + infinitive in the 1st person):

if I see her, I'll tell her

if you have finished that one, I'll give you another

There are three important exceptions:

* If the verb in the main clause is also in the present tense, an automatic or habitual result is normally implied. In such sentences **if** has the meaning of **when(ever)**:

if the sun shines, people look happier

if you're happy, then I'm happy

* When **will** is used also in the **if**-clause, the speaker refers to a person's willingness or intention to do something:

if you will kindly look this way, I'll try to explain the painter's approach

well if you will mix your drinks, what can you expect! (= if you will insist on . . .)

When this form is used to make requests the sentence can be made more polite by using **would**:

if you would be kind enough to look this way . . .

* When **should** is used in the **if**-clause (in all persons), the condition is implied to be less likely. Such **should**-clauses are often followed by the imperative, as in the first of the following examples:

if you should see him, please ask him to ring me

if they should not be there, you will have to manage by yourself

In a slightly more formal style **if** can be omitted and the sentence started with the subordinate clause with **should**:

should the matter arise again, telephone me at once

b) 'reality' less strong:

If the condition is expected not to take place or is in doubt or is opposed to known facts, the verb in the **if**-clause clause is in the past tense; the main clause has **would** (or **should** as well in the first person) + infinitive:

if I saw her, I would (I'd) tell her

if you had finished that one, I would give you another one

Note that this sentence-type need not always indicate a difference in the level of reality of a condition. Often there is little difference between it and the type in i) a) above:

if you tried harder, you would pass the exam (= if you try harder, you will pass the exam)

The use of the past tense may make the utterance a little friendlier or more polite.

ii) Reference to past time:

a) The condition did not take place. The verb of the subordinate clause is in the past perfect; the main clause has **would** (or **should** as well in the first person) + infinitive perfect:

if I had seen her, I would have told her

if you had finished that one, I would have given you another one

In a slightly more formal style **if** can be omitted and the subordinate clause started with **had**:

had I seen her, I would/should have told her

b) Exceptions:

* If the main clause refers to **present** unfulfilment of a past condition, **would** + infinitive (simple) can also be used:

if I had studied harder, I would be an engineer today (= if I had studied harder, I would have been an engineer today)

* The past tense is used in both clauses if, as in i)a above, an automatic or habitual result is implied (**if** = when(ever)):

if people had influenza in those days, they died

* If the condition is expected to have taken place, the restrictions on verb-form sequences in a) and b) above cease to apply. In such cases **if** often means 'as' or 'since':

if he was rude to you, why did you not walk out?

if he was rude to you, why have you still kept in touch?

if he was rude to you, why do you still keep in touch?

13 THE GERUND, THE INFINITIVE

The gerund, also known as a 'verbal noun' has the same form as the present participle (ending in **-ing**) but a different area of use. Some main points are:

i) As a noun:

driving is fun

smoking is not good for you

I love reading

ii) With characteristics of a verb (taking an object or complement or a subject):

writing this letter took me ages

being left-handed has never been a problem

the thought of Douglas doing that is absurd

iii) Being modified by an adverb:

it's a question of precisely defining our needs

iv) With a possessive:

Use of a possessive (my, his etc) before a gerund tends to be more written (formal) than spoken style:

we were suprised about you/your not being chosen

v) The gerund and the infinitive:

Sometimes either can be used after a verb:

I can't stand seeing him upset

I can't stand to see him upset

Sometimes there is an important difference:

we stopped having our rest at 3 o'clock (= ended it)
we stopped to have our rest at 3 o'clock (= started it)

Some common verbs which take the infinitive only are:

demand
expect
hope
want
wish

Some common verbs which take the gerund only are:

avoid
consider
dislike
enjoy
finish
keep
practise
risk

vi) The split infinitive:

An infinitive is said to be 'split' when an adverb is positioned between **to** and the verb:

they decided to reluctantly accept the offer

This is often considered bad style, the preferred version being:

they decided reluctantly to accept the offer

14 THE SUBJUNCTIVE

The subjunctive is identifiable by the omission of **-s** in the third person singular, by the use of **be** instead of **is** or the use of **were** instead of **was**. It is not particularly common in English. Some main uses are:

i) Set phrases expressing wishes:

long live the King!

God rest his soul

Heaven be praised

ii) The set phrase 'if need be':

well, if need be, you could always hire a car

iii) In clauses such as the following:

it is vital that he understand this

they recommended she sell the house

we propose that this new ruling be adopted

This use of the subjunctive is often found in more formal language. It is also commoner in spoken American English than in spoken British English.

iv) 'if I was/were':

Compare:
(a) **if I was in the wrong, it wasn't intentional**

(b) **if I were in the wrong, I would admit it**

In (a) the speaker is not casting any doubt on his/her having been in the wrong but is giving an explanation about the absence of intention. In (b), on the other hand, the speaker is not accepting as a fact that he/she was in the wrong; as far as the speaker is concerned this is still in doubt. Hence the use of the subjunctive **were**.

Sentence (b) could also be expressed using **was** and still have the same meaning. **Was** would here be rather more colloquial style than **were**.

15 MODAL AUXILIARIES

i) CAN-COULD

The contracted negative forms are **can't-couldn't**. The non-contracted present negative is **cannot**.

a) ability (= be able to):

can machines 'think'?

I can explain that

when I was a student I could explain that sort of thing easily

For other tenses it is common to use forms of **be able to**:

I used to be able to explain that sort of thing easily

I'll be able to tell you the answer tomorrow

I've never been able to understand her

Note that in conditional clauses **could** + simple infinitive refers to the present or future (compare **would** under Expressing Conditions, p 36):

you could do a lot better if you'd only try

b) permission:

can/could I have a look at your photos?

Note that **could** refers as much to the present or future as **can**. The only difference is that **could** is a little more tentative or polite. For example, a child is unlikely to say:

could I go out and play?

Could can sometimes be used for past permission when the context is clearly in the past:

for some reason we couldn't smoke in the lounge yesterday; but today we can

Otherwise, and for other tenses, use the forms of **be allowed to**:

we weren't allowed to see him, he was so ill

will they be allowed to change the rules?

c) possibility:

that can't be right

what shall I do? – you can always talk to a lawyer/you could talk to a lawyer

Note that **could** does not refer to the past but to the present or future. If the reference to the past has to be made, **could** must be followed by the infinitive perfect:

you could have talked to a lawyer

I know I could have, but I didn't want to

* **Could** and **may** are sometimes interchangeable in referring to possibility:

you could/may be right

But there is sometimes an important difference between **can** and **may** in their reference to possibility:

(a) **your comments can be overheard**

(b) **your comments may be overheard**

(a) says that it is possible to overhear the comments (eg because they are very loud) whether or not it is likely that anybody actually will. (b) says that there is some likelihood that the comments will actually be overheard.

This difference is also seen in negative uses:

don't worry, he can't have heard us (= it is impossible for him to have heard us)

by the look on his face, he may not have heard us (= it is possible that he did not hear us)

d) (**could** only) suggestions:

you could try speaking a little more slowly

they could always sell their second house if they need money

e) (**could** only) reproach, annoyance:

you could have told me I had paint on my face!

ii) MAY-MIGHT

Contracted form **mayn't** not common in the 'permission' use of **may**; instead **may not** or **must not/mustn't** are used. The contracted negative of **might** is **mightn't**.

a) permission:

may I open a window? – no, you may not!

The use of **may** implies a slightly more polite request etc than the use of **can**. A speaker who uses **might** to express permission is being extremely polite:

I wonder if I might have another of those cakes

might I suggest we stop there for today?

Note that **might** refers to the present or future. It very rarely refers to the past when used in a main clause. Compare:

he then asked if he might smoke (might in subordinate clause)

he then asked if he was allowed to smoke

and

he wasn't allowed to smoke

Might is not possible in the last example; forms of **be allowed to** are used instead.

b) possibility:

it may/might be still be possible
they may/might change their minds
it mayn't/mightn't be necessary after all
she may/might have left a note upstairs

c) (normally **might**) surprise, annoyance etc:

and who may/might you be?
and what might that be supposed to mean?

d) (**might** only) suggestions:

they might at least apologize
you might like to try one of these cigars

Note that this use often hovers on the verge of being an imperative:

you might take this down the road to your Gran
you might like to read the next chapter for Monday

e) (**might** only) reproach, annoyance:

you might have told me he was deaf!
they might have written back to us at least!

f) wishes:

may you have a very happy retirement
may all your dreams come true!
may you be forgiven for telling such lies!

This use is normally confined to fixed expressions or is rather rhetorical or literary.

iii) MUST-HAD TO

The contracted negative form is **mustn't** (for **have** see p 30).

a) obligation:

we have no choice, we must do what he wants

must you go already?

It is also possible to use **have to**, or the more colloquial **have got to**:

we have no choice, we have (got) to do what he says

do you have to go already/have you got to go already?

Often the meaning is the same. But in cases where some external obligation is implied (eg someone else has told you to do something) **have to** is more often used:

I have to be there for my interview at 10 o'clock

For the past and future use **have to**:

we had to do what he wanted

I'll have to finish it tomorrow

b) negatives:

i) **Must not** is used to express prohibition, what is forbidden:

you mustn't drink and drive

ii) **Don't have to** or **haven't got to** are used to express a lack of obligation:

we don't have to drive all night, we could always stop off at a hotel

For the past tense of i) use **be allowed to**:

when we were children we weren't allowed to . . .

The past tense of ii) is straightforward:

you didn't have to buy one, you could have used mine

c) probability:

hello, you must be Susan

that must be my mistake

she must have been surprised to see you

Have to is often used in this sense too:

you have to be kidding!

and so is **have got to**, especially in British English:

well if she said so, it's got to be true (it's = it has)

iv) OUGHT TO

The contracted negative is **oughtn't to**. The infinitive after **ought** has **to** in contrast to other modal auxiliaries.

a) obligation:

Ought to is similar in meaning to **should** in its sense of obligation:

you oughtn't even to think things like that

and he ought to know!

But **ought to** is less emphatic than **must** in these senses. Compare:

I must/have to avoid fatty foods (firm obligation or necessity)

I ought to avoid fatty foods (less intense obligation)

Must or **have (got) to** normally replace **ought to** in questions:

must you/do you have to/have you got to visit your mother every Sunday?

b) probability:

she ought to be halfway to Rome by now

£50? – that ought to be enough

v) SHALL-SHOULD

The contracted negative forms are **shan't- shouldn't**.
For conditional sentences see p 36.
For talking about the future see p 58.

a) (**should** only) obligation (often moral):

you should take more exercise

you shouldn't talk to her like that

what do you think I should do?

something was obviously not quite as it should be

with a new fuse fitted it should work

b) (**should** only) probability:

it's after ten, they should be in Paris by now

if doing one took you two hours, then three shouldn't take longer than six hours, should it?

is it there? – well, it should be because that's where I left it

c) (**should** only) in tentative statements (**would** is commoner):

I should just like to say that . . .

I should hardly call him a great innovative mind but . . .

d) expressing surprise, annoyance:

there was a knock at the door, and who should it be but . . .

where's the money gone? – how should I know?

e) (**shall** only) in legal or official language:

these sums shall be payable monthly

as shall be stipulated by the contract

the bearings shall have a diameter of no less than . . .

vi) WILL-WOULD

The contracted negative forms are **won't-wouldn't**.

For conditional sentences see p 36.
For talking about the future see p 58.

a) To describe natural ability, capacity, inclination or characteristic behaviour:

concrete will not normally float (doesn't float)

the paint will normally last for two to three years

the tank will hold about 50 litres

leave him alone and he'll play for hours

they will keep getting it wrong! (annoyance)

the car won't start on damp mornings

Would is used to refer to the past:

leave him alone and he would play for hours

they would insist on calling me 'pet'

I lost it – you would!, that's typical of you!

b) To express commands or emphasize insistence:

you will do as you are told!

he will (damn well) do as he's told!

will you stop that right now!

I will not tolerate this!

c) To appeal to somebody's memory or knowledge (rather formal language):

you will remember the point at which we left off last week's seminar

as you will all doubtless be aware, there have been rumours recently that . . .

d) To express assumption:

there's someone at the door – that'll be Graham

how old is he now? – he'll be about 45

e) Asking questions, offering:

will you have another cup? – thank you, I will

won't you try some of these?

did they ask you if you would like to try one?

f) Making requests:

will/would you move your car, please?

The 'would' form is more polite, less direct.

OTHER AUXILIARIES

vii) USED TO

Used to can be regarded as a kind of auxiliary, since the use of **do** is optional:

he used not to smoke so much

he didn't use to smoke so much

did you use to know him?

used you to know him?

In the second pair of examples the first form is commoner in spoken English.

viii) DARE, NEED

These verbs can behave either as ordinary verbs or as modal auxiliaries. As auxiliaries, they take no **-s** in the 3rd person singular present tense; **do** is not used in questions and negations; and a following infinitive is without **to**.

a) as ordinary verbs:

I don't dare to say anything

would/do you dare to ask him?

you don't need to ask first

do I need to sign it?

b) as modal auxiliaries:

I daren't say anything

dare you ask him?

you needn't ask first

need I sign it?

* **Dare** can be half an ordinary verb (eg with **do** in questions and negations) and half an auxiliary (followed by an infinitive without **to**):

I don't dare say anything

* In main clauses that are not questions or negations **need** can only be an ordinary verb:

I need to go to the toilet

ix) HAVE, GET

Have or **get** can be used in a 'causative' way as follows:

we're going to have/get the car resprayed

I can't do it myself but I can have/get it done for you

The action is not performed by the speaker personally; rather the speaker **gets** someone else to do it.

16 TALKING ABOUT THE PRESENT

i) The present simple is used:

a) For habitual or general events or states of affairs:

I have a shower in the mornings
she works for an insurance company
where do you buy your shoes?
where do you come from?
what do I do when the computer bleeps at me?
the earth goes round the sun

b) With verbs expressing general mental states, desire, dislike, point of view, or referring to the senses:

I (dis)like/love/hate/want that girl
I believe/suppose/think/imagine he's right
we hear/see/feel/perceive the world around us
what's that I smell?

ii) The present continuous is used:

a) To refer to ongoing, normally temporary, events or states of affairs:

what are you doing up there?
I'm trying to find my old passport I left here
at the moment it's being used as a spare bedroom
what are you thinking about?

b) To express an attitude (usually of displeasure, amusement or surprise) towards something:

he's always mixing our names up (annoyance, amusement etc)
he's always losing his car keys
you're always saying that!
you're not going out looking like that!

iii) Present simple and present continuous contrasted:

I live in London (simple)

I'm living in London (continuous)

The second sentence implies that the speaker is not permanently based in London, that living there is only temporary. The first sentence refers to a permanent state of affairs.

I have a shower every morning (simple)

I'm having a shower every morning (these days) (continuous)

The second sentence implies that having a regular morning shower is only a temporary state of affairs, something that is being done at the moment (and that might not last). The first sentence, in the present simple, has no such implication of a restriction in time.

she works for an insurance company

she's working for an insurance company

The difference is less emphasized in this pair. But the first example could not refer to a temporary state of affairs. The second example could refer to either a temporary or permanent state of affairs.

There are cases where there is really no difference between simple and continuous:

how are you feeling this morning?

how do you feel this morning?

17 TALKING ABOUT THE PAST

i) The past simple:

This is used for completed actions or events in the past:

he got up and left the room

broken again? – I only fixed it yesterday!

in what year did the Rolling Stones first have a hit?

ii) Used to/would:

These are used for habitual or recurring events or actions in the past:

we always used to have fish on Fridays

on Fridays we would have fish

iii) The past continuous:

This stresses the continuity of an action or event:

I was living in Germany when that happened

sorry, could you say that again? – I wasn't listening

what were you doing out in the garden last night?

I was having supper when he came home

Past simple and past continuous are often used to pick out the relationship of two events to each other in the past, or to highlight the way in which the speaker/writer wishes to present them. In the last example above a single event (he came home) is contrasted with an ongoing event (I was having supper). Compare this with:

I had supper when he was coming home

This sentence is quite different. The ongoing or continuous aspect has been shifted to 'he was coming home'. 'I had supper' refers to something that took place at some point in time during the course of the continuous event of 'coming home'.

Compare also:

I was having supper while he was coming home

In this sentence the point of view has been shifted again to present the events as two parallel ongoing events.

iv) The present perfect(ive):

a) This is used for past actions or events that have some relevance for the present:

I've read nearly all of Somerset Maugham's books

I have never read any of Somerset Maugham's books

Both these sentences describe the present state of one's reading as regards Somerset Maugham's books.

Compare these with:

I read one of Maugham's novels on holiday last year

This sentence describes one completed event in the past.

Some more useful comparisons:

have you seen him this morning? (said while it is still morning)

did you see him this morning? (said in the afternoon or evening)

b) The continuous form can be used to stress the continuity of an action or state of affairs:

what have you been reading recently?

we haven't seen you for ages, where have you been keeping yourself?

what have you been saying to him?

I've been meaning to ask you something, doctor

Although sometimes there is little actual difference in meaning between simple and continuous:

I've been living here for 15 years (continuous)

I've lived here for 15 years (simple)

Note the use of **since** when the reference is to a point in time:

I've been living here since 1972

The difference in use between simple and continuous can sometimes be quite subtle:

I've been waiting for you here for a whole hour!

I've waited for you here for a whole hour!

Of these two examples the first could be said when the person eventually arrived. The second could not, since it implies that the waiting has finished.

v) The past perfect(ive):

a) This is used to describe actions or events or states of affairs in the past that took place or were the case before other happenings in the past. It expresses one past time in relation to another past time:

the fire had already been put out when they got there

he searched the directory but the file had been erased the day before

had you heard of him before you came here?

they hadn't left anything in the fridge so I went out to eat

It can also be used to imply the cessation of a state of affairs (especially mental states):

I had hoped to speak to him this morning

This implies that the chance of speaking to him is now perceived as being very slight or as having ceased to exist.

b) To stress continuity the continuous form can be used:

I'd been wanting to ask that question myself

had you been waiting long before they arrived?

For the past perfect(ive) in clauses of condition, see p 37–38.

18 TALKING ABOUT THE FUTURE

i) **Will** and **shall**:

a) When referring to the future in the 1st person **will** or **shall** can be used. Both can be contracted to **'ll**. **Shall**, however, is mainly British English:

I will/I'll/I shall let you know as soon as I can

we won't/shan't need that many

b) In other persons **will** is used:

you'll be sorry!

lunch will take about another ten minutes

they'll just have to wait

c) If the speaker is expressing an intention in the 2nd or 3rd person (often as a promise or threat), **shall** is sometimes found, but is no longer as common as **will**:

you shall be treated just like the others

they shall pay for this!

If the intention or willingness is not the speaker's, **will ('ll)** is used:

he will/he'll do it, I'm sure

d) **Shall** is used to make suggestions:

shall we make a start?

e) **Will** can be used to make requests:

will you come with me please?

f) Offering, making statements about the immediate future:

In the following examples **will** is used rather than **shall** (although the contracted form **'ll** is much commoner):

that's ok, I'll do it

I'll have a beer please

that's the door bell – ok, I'll get it

ii) Future simple and future continuous:

a) **Will** and **shall** followed by the continuous may be used to stress continuity of action:

what will (what'll) you be doing this time next year?

b) Compare the following:

will you speak to him about it? (simple)

will you be speaking to him about it? (continuous)

The use of the continuous in the second example makes it clear that the speaker is not making a direct request (as in the first example) but that he/she is merely making a factual enquiry as to whether the person spoken to intends to 'speak to him about it'.

iii) **Be going to**:

a) This is often used in the same way as **will**:

will it ever stop raining?

is it ever going to stop raining?

b) **Be going to** is commoner than **will** or **shall** in statements of intention:

I'm going to take them to court

they're going to buy a new car

But in a longer sentence containing other adverbials and clauses **will** is also possible:

listen, what we'll do is this, we'll make him think that we've left, then we'll come back in through the back door and . . .

c) **Be going to** is used in preference to **will** when the reasons for the statement made about the future relate directly to the present:

I know what he's going to say (it's written all over his face)

iii) The present simple:

a) This can be used to refer to the future when a fixed programme of events is referred to or is implied:

when does the race start?

the match kicks off at 2.30

As the second example above shows, it is particularly common when used together with an adverb of time:

we go on holiday tomorrow

the plane leaves at 7.30

b) The present simple is normally used in adverbial clauses of time or condition:

you'll be surprised when you see her

if the sun shines, I'll be truly amazed

Note: this type of **when**- and **if**-clause should not be confused with interrogative clauses in which **when** means 'at what time?' and **if** means 'whether', for example:

does he know when they're arriving? (when are they arriving?)

I don't know if he'll agree (will he agree?)

iv) The present continuous:

a) The present continuous is often used in a way similar to **be going to** in expressing intention:

I'm putting you in charge of exports (= I'm going to put you in charge of exports)

what are you doing for your holidays? (= what are you going to do for your holidays?)

But note a subtle difference between the following:

I'm taking him to court

I'm going to take him to court

The first example is more definite than the second, less open to doubt or revision. The second could be construed as less of an established fact.

b) The present continuous can also be used to imply pre- arrangement in the future in a way similar to **will** + infinitive continuous or the present simple:

he's giving a concert tomorrow

c) And it can also be used in a way similar to the present simple when referring especially to scheduled events in the future:

when are they coming?

they're arriving at Heathrow at midnight

v) **Be to**:

Be to is often used to express specific plans for the future, especially plans made for us by other people or by fate:

all the guests are to be present by 7.30

I'm to report to a Mr Glover on Tuesday

are we ever to meet again, I wonder?

vi) **Be about to:**

This is used to express the imminent future:

please take your seats, the play is about to begin

Particularly in American English it is also used to express one's intentions about the future:

I'm not about to sign a contract like that!

In such cases British English would be more likely to use **be going to**.

vii) The future perfect(ive):

a) This is used to talk about a completed event in the future:

by the time you get there we will have finished dinner

b) It is also used for assumptions:

I expect you'll have been wondering why I asked you here

19 PHRASAL VERB PARTICLES

This section looks at phrasal verbs from the particle point of view and examines a wide range of particles used to create phrasal verbs. Each of these particles is divided into its main senses or types of usage with a short definition. In addition to this a number of typical examples of usage for each sense area are given.

ABOUT

1. movement in all directions, sometimes suggesting confusion:

the bloodhounds cast about for a fresh scent; I felt about for the light switch; the pain of his wounds made him lash about; I was rushing about trying to get ready when the phone rang; people milled about in the streets; I wish you would stop fussing about

2. having nothing specific to do:

I hate standing about at street corners, so make sure you're on time; she always keeps me hanging about when we arrange to meet

3. being in the general area:

make sure there's nobody about before you force the window; he looked about for a taxi

4. on the subject of:

what do you think about his latest film?; they know a lot about antiques; are his books known about over here?; what's he rambling on about now?

ACROSS

1. from one side to the other:

we walked across the railway lines

2. on or to the opposite side, often of a street:

always help old ladies across busy roads; I'm just popping across for a newspaper

3. comprehension, understanding:

he finds it hard to put his ideas across; how can I get it across to them that it's important to keep copies of all your files?

AFTER

1. following:

the boy was running after his ball and just dashed out into the road; there she is at the corner – send someone after her

2. searching for:

the police are after him

3. finding out how someone is:

nurse, if anyone calls to enquire after Mr Thompson, tell them he's resting comfortably

4. being like an older member of the family:

my niece takes after me

AGAINST

1. touching:

the cat startled me, brushing against me in the dark hall

2. opposition:

I'm against capital punishment; she always kicked against the idea of marriage

3. protection:

fluoride is said to guard against tooth decay

4. something being a disadvantage:

will the fact that he has a previous conviction go against him?

AHEAD

1. in front:

the favourite has got ahead now and looks likely to win; look straight ahead please

2. success:

you will never get ahead unless you are conscientious; why do you think you have kept ahead of the competition all these years?; the project is moving ahead nicely

3. the future:

looking ahead to the next budget . . .; it is essential to plan ahead

ALONG

1. movement the length of something:

he walked along the street in a daze, the road runs along the river bank

2. progress:

we were driving along when suddenly . . .; we were tearing along at a hundred miles an hour; things are coming along nicely; how's she coming along at school?; the work is just chugging along at a pretty slow pace

3. departure:

I'll have to be beetling along if I want to catch my train; I'll be getting along now then (ie leaving); the police told the crowd to move along

4. coping:

how do old age pensioners manage to rub along on so little money?

5. dismissing someone, often impatiently:

get along with you!; she told the children to run along and play

6. accompanying other people:

why not bring your sister along?; he's going to have to drag his little brother along

7. to a place not very far away and often on the same street:

my mother sent me along to see how you were

APART

1. being separated:

the two fighters had to be dragged apart; I saw them draw apart as I entered the room; I can't get these two pieces apart

2. being in parts:

he says it just came apart in his hands; the police pulled the flat apart looking for drugs

3. aside:

the doctor drew the parents apart; joking apart, what do you really think?

4. being different:

what sets her apart from all the other children in my class is . . .; he stands apart from the others because of his very placid temperament

AROUND

1. in different places:

you have to dig around for that kind of information; I'm hunting around for a pen that works

2. having nothing specific to do:

how much longer do we have to wait around before he arrives?

3. in the general area:

he's around somewhere – have you looked in the kitchen?

ASIDE

1. to the side:

please step aside and let us pass; they moved the old wardrobe aside to reveal . . .

2. leading someone away to ensure privacy:

the teacher called him aside to ask how his father was; he drew her aside for a moment

3. saving something to be dealt with or used later:

leaving that question aside for the moment . . .; could you lay that aside and work on this instead?; I have some money put aside if you need it

AT

1. a certain place:

I called at your mother's this morning but she wasn't in; this train will call at Preston and Carlisle; how many stations did you stop at?

2. towards, in the direction of:

the bearers chopped at the undergrowth with their machetes; don't clutch at my hand like that; he hinted at the possibility of a promotion; the birds were picking at the crumbs

AWAY

1. departure, or being absent:

I'm sorry but he has been called away on some important business; he drove away in a taxi; he ran away into the crowd

2. being or putting at a distance:

the child backed away from the dog; something must be done to get her away from their influence; why do you move away whenever I touch you?

3. continuing to do something for some time:

let the mixture boil away for five minutes; teenagers chewing away at gum . . .; she's pegging away at her maths; well, keep asking away until you get an answer; there he was, snoring away on the sofa; they just sat there giggling away; she was in the bath, singing away; he lay groaning away on the ground

4. removing or disposing of something, often unwanted:

I want you to brush those leaves away from the path; maybe someone with a van could cart the wardrobe away; she rubbed the dirt away from the window; if you don't want it fling it away

5. storing something:

I wouldn't be surprised if he had salted away a fair bit in his time (ie put away some money for future use); lock it away where it'll be safe; he keeps it stored away in the attic

6. disappearing:

the water has all boiled away; he is wasting away with grief; the water gradually trickled away; he slowly rubbed the old paint away

7. using something up:

he has drunk his entire wages away

8. the start of an action

could I ask some questions? – sure, fire away

BACK

1. movement towards the rear:

she flung back her hair; move your men back, Lieutenant

2. returning:

flood waters are receding and people are beginning to filter back to their homes; it's so cold I think I'll head back; she's being moved back to Personnel Department; I'll send it back to you in the post

3. doing something again:

she asked her secretary to read the letter back; we've bought back our old house; could you play that bit back? (ie on tape)

4. retreating or withdrawing:

the intense heat forced them back; the plant will die back in autumn but give you a lovely show again in summer

5. being delayed or made slower:

rein your horse back or you'll be in trouble; the pilot throttled back and came in to land

6. lessening something:

this old rose bush needs to be chopped back; we'll have to cut back on our expenses; we trimmed back the hedge a bit

7. withholding or repressing:

I forced back my tears; what are you keeping back from us?

BEHIND

1. being at the back of something:

the wall they were hiding behind gave way; his wife always walks behind

2. being delayed, not up to date:

the landlady says we're getting behind with the rent; if you're slipping behind with the payments/your work . . .

3. being in an inferior position, losing:

he was behind right from the start; you're dropping badly behind with your work

4. forgetting or not taking, not going:

do you mind being left behind to look after the children?; that's ok, you go on ahead, I'll stay behind

BY

1. going past:

we had to push by a lot of people; the cars raced by; time goes by so fast, doesn't it?

2. according or with reference to:

my mother swears by castor oil; which theory do you go by?

3. visiting a place casually or quickly:

I've just dropped by for a minute; come by some time; I'll pop by to see you one day; we stopped by at the art gallery on the way home

DOWN

1. movement from above:

the sun blazed down on their bare heads; call Tom down for tea (eg from upstairs); she dropped down from the tree; pass me down that big plate from the top shelf

2. toward the ground or a lower position:

I bent down to pick up the old man's stick; the hurricane blew down hundreds of mature trees; he drew her down beside him on the couch; draw the blinds down

3. recording something for future reference:

could someone mark down the main points?; I've got it down in my notebook; I could see him scribbling something down

4. ending something:

the audience hooted the proposal down; it was voted down; they all shouted the speaker down

5. securing or making something safe or tight:

we have to chain the garden furniture down or it would vanish overnight; screw the lid down properly; they tied him down on the ground; glue it down

6. stopping a vehicle in some way:

we waved a taxi down

7. passing from one generation to another:

the necklace has been passed down from mother to daughter for centuries; an old folksong which has come down though the centuries

8. something being reduced or diminishing:

all the prices in the shop have been marked down; thin the sauce down with a little milk if necessary; you're going too fast, slow down; the pilot eased down on the throttle

9. something not working:

the computer is down again; she broke down and wept

10. strictness or authority:

the police are clamping down on licence-dodgers; the teacher really came down on me for not having learnt the dates properly; the court is going to hand down its sentence tomorrow

11. consuming food or drink:

if you don't force some food down you'll collapse; the dog gobbled it all down in a second; she absolutely wolfed her dinner down; come on now, drink this down

FOR

1. having something as its target or object:

with all this overtime she's doing, she must be bucking for promotion; she felt in her bag for the keys; stop fishing for compliments!; the qualities looked for in candidates are . . .

2. in favour of:

he argued strongly for a return to the traditional methods of teaching grammar; the points of view argued for in this paper

FORTH

1. going out, especially to face an adversary:

the Saracens sallied forth to engage the infidel in hand to hand combat (old-fashioned in this usage); he sallied forth to face the waiting fans (humorous usage)

2. producing:

Mary brought forth a son (old-fashioned or biblical); the shrub puts forth the most gloriously scented blossom

3. speaking for a long time, often pompously:

he is always holding forth about something; she spouted forth about the benefits of free enterprise

FORWARD

1. movement towards the front:

please come forward one by one as I call your names; the cat edged forward to the corner of the lawn where the bird was sitting; bring your chair forward

2. looking to the future with anticipation:

we're really looking forward to seeing them again; that's something I am definitely not looking forward to; looking forward to hearing from you (polite conclusion to business letter)

3. an earlier time:

the chairman has decided to bring the board meeting forward a week

4. presenting something for consideration:

does anyone have any other suggestions they wish to bring forward?; the theory that he puts forward in his book

FROM

the point of departure, origination:

we'll be flying from Heathrow; where did you fly from?; where did you spring from? (ie appear suddenly); where do babies come from?; they come from Ghana (ie are Ghanaians); they will be coming from Ghana next week (ie arriving)

HOME

1. the place where one lives:

who is taking you home?; I'll see you home safely; go home

2. inserting something in the proper place and as deeply as possible:

make sure you hammer the nails home; is the plug pushed home properly?

3. causing someone to understand or appreciate something:

did you drive it home to them that they must be back by midnight?; the recent accident brought home to them very forcefully the need for insurance; that comment really hit home (ie had strong effect)

IN

1. movement from outside:

the cat was a stray who just wandered in one day; there's no need to burst in like that; we crept in so as not to disturb you; don't stand so close to the edge of the pool – you might fall in

2. being or being put somewhere:

I think it was a bad idea to leave that bit in the letter; you shouldn't have left it in; I'm going to the bank to pay these cheques in; he poked his finger in; the car's pretty full but we could squeeze one more in

3. being confined or closed:

when the police arrived they found he had barricaded himself in; women at home with children often feel fenced in; help! I'm locked in!; the old doorway was bricked in

4. adding something to something else:

fold in the flour; then, of course, Dad had to chime in with his suggestions; rake in some fertiliser; these extra ideas which the director of the film built in are not found in the original novel; a new character was then written in to the series

5. arriving or coming near:

members of the orchestra eventually began to filter in; when the train pulled in; as I looked out of the window I saw a car drive in

6. completing something:

fill in this form; he sketched in the features

7. being at home or receiving into one's home:

will you be in this evening?; you've bought in enough tins to last a lifetime; let's invite the people next door in for a drink

8. delivering or surrendering something:

the wanted man handed himself in to the police; give your essays in tomorrow; when do you need this work in by?

9. ending:

I'm jacking my job in; pack that noise in!; the engine's packed in

10. something being completely destroyed:

they had to beat the door in since nobody had a key; the roof fell in, showering the firemen with debris

11. making something narrower or tighter:

I asked my dressmaker to take the sleeves in; pull the rope in a bit to get rid of the slack; hold your stomach in

INTO

1. movement from outside:

don't just barge into the room – knock first; the operator cut into our conversation; I could see into the room and there was nobody there; the Fraud Squad is enquiring into the affair

2. using part of, often in a negative sense:

we're going to have to break into our savings to pay for the repairs to the roof; it cuts into our time too much

3. coming in contact with something or somebody:

if you looked where you were going you wouldn't keep barging into people; some idiot running for a train cannoned into me

OFF

1. removing something or somebody:

don't bite it off – use the scissors; it took ages to scrape the old paint off; he was carted off in a police car; we're going to have to force the lid off

2. departure:

the car slowly moved off; the boys beetled off when they saw the local bobby approaching; don't hurry off – stay and have some tea; he just wandered off down the road and I never saw him again

3. leaving a vehicle of some kind:

as the bus slowed, he jumped off; the doors opened and everyone piled off; let's hop off here; come on, hop off, let me have a go on your bike

4. ending or disconnecting something:

put the lights off please; he choked off my screams with a gag; he has sworn off alcohol

5. something declining in volume, quality etc:

don't touch the soup until it has cooled off a bit; this meat has gone off; attendances have fallen off

6. as an intensifier, indicating completeness:

the script writers have decided to kill this character off; the detective was bought off (ie bribed); most of the land has been sold off

7. beginning something:

let me start off by saying . . .; who's going to lead off with the first question?; the procession moved off

8. being on holiday:

can I have next week off please?; they gave him a couple of days off

9. something being inaccessible:

the street has been barricaded off because of a gas leak; for reasons of safety, that part of the road has been closed off; they have divided some of the rooms off in an attempt to save on heating costs; this part has been partitioned off from the rest of the room; the rubbish dump has been walled off

ON

1. continuing:

read on to the end of the chapter; they just chatted on for hours; she worked on into the night; I think I'll work on a little longer; he ran on despite the cries for him to stop; shall we stroll on then?; they climbed on until the light failed; he slept on in spite of the noise around him

2. referring to clothes or something similar:

he whipped a dressing gown on and went to answer the door; the police clapped handcuffs on the thief; what did he have on?; it was too small, I couldn't get it on

4. an electrical appliance or something similar functioning:

do you know that you've left the headlights on?; turn the TV on, would you?

5. using something as a basis:

what do the animals feed (up)on in winter?; all cars should run on unleaded petrol; what sort on fuel does it run on?; she thrives (up)on hard work; that wasn't something I'd planned on

6. being in a vehicle or aircraft:

the train stopped and everybody piled on; they couldn't get any more passengers on; how many passengers are allowed on?

7. something being attached or fastened:

the lid hooks on; where does this bit fit on?; he latches on to anyone who looks well off; it seemed like an excellent idea and we seized (up)on it immediately

8. bringing forward or advancing:

the crowd is clapping her on as she reaches the last mile; he wanted to look in the car show room but I hurried him on; the jockey's having to whip the horse on

9. something that is arranged or scheduled to happen:

I've got something on every night next week; what's on TV tonight?

10. something being transferred:

she handed your book on to me; could you pass the news on?

OUT

1. movement from inside:

they bolted out of the door; she drove out of the garage; he said a few words and then hurried out; I'm popping out to the library

2. being expelled or excluded:

that tree will have to come down, it's blocking out all the sun; I've flung out that old jacket of yours; deal me out of this game, it's about time I went home; heavy floods have driven thousands of people out of their homes; go and rout him out of bed; they have a knack of freezing out people they don't like; I feel a bit left out

3. leaving:

the train had only just pulled out when . . .; he walked out on his wife and kids; I've had enough of this relationship, I'm getting out

4. distributing:

we need volunteers to hand out leaflets; who's going to deal out the cards?

5. stretching:

he held out his hand in a pleading gesture; reach out your glass; you can pull the elastic out to twice its length

6. removing:

is it time to take the cake out? (ie out of the oven); don't push me out of the way; a lot of the pages have been ripped out; we had a bit of an argument about it but I finally screwed some money out of him

7. solving a problem or difficult situation:

I couldn't get the equation to work out; things just didn't pan out between us; it all came out right in the end

8. loud noises:

stop barking out orders like a sergeant major; the loudspeakers were blaring out the candidate's message; she cried out in pain; speak out clearly please

9. a light or something similar being extinguished:

the fire has gone out; he was knocked out in the first round; he butted his cigar out in the ashtray; switch the light out in the garage

10. extricating something or someone, often with difficulty:

how did you get out of doing your homework?; I wish I could wriggle out of this visit to my in-laws

11. outdoors, not at home:

the soldiers camped out in the fields; it was such a beautiful night we said the children could sleep out (ie in the open); I've been invited out for lunch; is he in or is he out?

12. making something bigger, wider etc:

I left the dress to be let out at the seams; your essay needs to be fleshed out; the speech was rounded out with some statistics on the company's performance in the last year

OVER

1. going from one side to another:

she walked over the railway bridge; he saw me on the other pavement and hurried over; hey, move over, there's room for two in this bed!; I'll fly over and see you; they plan to bring witnesses over from France to testify

2. going a short distance:

I'll drive over and see you soon; our neighbours are having us over for dinner on Saturday night

3. transferring:

we've switched over to another paper; I don't like this programme, could you change over?

4. turning something:

he folded over the letter so that I couldn't see the signature; fork the ground over thoroughly before planting

5. communicating a feeling, intention, impression etc:

it is very difficult to get over to men how women feel about rape; they need to find a better way of putting their company image over; they come over as being rather arrogant; how did they come over to you?

6. position directly above:

he bent over the balcony for a better look; with this threat hanging over him ...

7. covering completely:

skies are expected to cloud over later in the day; the horrible realization that I was not alone crept over me; the lake rarely freezes over; the door was papered over many years ago; the beautiful old floorboards have been carpeted over

8. remaining:

the film has proved so popular that it is being held over for another two weeks; there's quite a lot left over

9. being finished or done thoroughly:

the party was over by midnight; just check over the names on the guest list; be sure to read your essay over before handing it in

10. going beyond its proper boundaries:

the milk has boiled over; the river flooded over into the streets; the water was all spilling over

11. falling:

she was knocked over by a bus; she tumbled over; over he went with a crash!

PAST

passing someone or something:

he brushed past me in the street; we had just gone past the shop when . . . ; cars raced past; time just flies past; he just casually strolled on past

ROUND

(especially British English)

1. movement of circular kind:

thoughts were spinning round in her head; you must hand your sweets round

2. forming a circle:

a crowd gathered round to watch; they all crowded round

3. different places or parts of one place:

we went round the art gallery; would you like to see round the house?; were you able to see round?; I'll phone round and see if anyone else knows about it; could you ask round?

4. moving something or making it face the other way:

I've been bumping into things ever since your mother changed all the furniture round; he turned the car round and went home

5. one's home, when referring to people who live or work not very far away:

could you call round tomorrow morning, doctor?; they always go out when their son has some of his friends round; drop round some time; let's invite them round

THROUGH

1. in at one side and out the other:

we strolled through the old part of the city; the policeman came bursting through the door, gun at the ready; he looked through me as if I didn't exist; we had to plough through snowdrifts; we're not stopping here, just passing through

2. penetrating something:

the crowd broke through the barriers; the sun is expected to break through sometime this morning; supplies are filtering through; you're wearing your jumper through at the elbows; the soles of my boots are almost worn through

3. success or accomplishment:

she brought all of us through the exam; we'll just have to muddle through without her; don't worry, I'll see you through; he was very ill but he's pulled through; his teachers pushed him through; against all the odds they fought through

4. something being done thoroughly:

they went through everyone's hand luggage; will you read through my speech and give me your opinion?; I'll be up all night wading through this paperwork; have these bags been looked through yet?; it has to be read through twice; it had obviously been checked through in some detail; it hasn't been properly thought through

5. ending something:

I'm through with men!; let me know when you get through with what you're doing

TO

1. movement towards:

name the foreign countries you've travelled to

2. being conscious:

when do you think they'll have brought him to?

3. in connection with:

what do you say to this suggestion?; who are you talking to?; has your letter been replied to yet?; are you being attended to, madam?

4. close:

could you push the door to a little?

TOGETHER

acting as or forming a group or whole:

we always gathered together for morning prayers; let's collect some of the neighbours together and talk about it; you must keep the group together and not let people wander off on their own; what were just vague ideas are coming together into a definite proposal; he's really got it together (ie is successful)

TOWARDS

(American English **toward**)

1. in the direction of:

he started walking towards the bridge; my husband wants a holiday in Spain but I'm leaning towards France

2. in a position facing:

the castle looks towards the sea; the street which it looks towards

3. about, in relation to:

how does she really feel towards him?

4. doing or using something for a purpose:

I'd like to start saving towards my retirement; put that money towards a new car

UNDER

1. beneath something:

when the sirens sounded, we always used to get under the table; fold the edges under; the sides of the carpet are folded back and tacked under with staples

2. governing or ruling something:

under the terms of the new law . . .; that information comes under the Official Secrets Act

3. suppressing:

a military government held the country under for many years; the government is doing its best to keep the rebels under

4. being in a certain category:

I'm looking for books on garden design – what subject do they come under in the catalogue?; what should I look under? – vegetables or fruit?

UP

1. movement from beneath:

hand that hammer up so I don't have to get off the step ladder; pass the suitcases up; the climbers struggled slowly on up

2. to the floor above, upstairs:

carry this tray up to your father; do you know where his room is or do you want me to see you up?; let's invite our neighbours up for coffee

3. lifting:

he picked up his bags and left; bet you can't lift that up; she hitched up her skirt and started to run; I'll just finish pinning up this hem; hold your head up

4. getting to one's feet or to an upright position:

I jumped up to protest; they all stood up; the old man sat up in bed with a start; don't slouch, straighten up your shoulders

5. approaching:

old age has crept up; the manager of the shop rushed up to ask if he could be of assistance; he wandered up to us

6. getting better:

business is looking up; the weather has cleared up

7. an increase in amount, power, volume etc:

this has forced house prices up; turn the television up, I must be going deaf; he's juicing up the engine of his car; the fire blazed up, catching them by surprise; let me plump up your pillows; why did they tart the pub up? – I liked it the way it was

8. finding or collecting something:

she bundled up her clothes and beat a hasty retreat; I'm going to have to gen up on the latest fashions; he wants me to hunt up his ancestors; where can I pick up a taxi?; do you think you can rake up enough money for the deposit?; where did you dig up that story?

9. supporting something:

can anyone back your story up?; a street of shored-up buildings; what's it held up by?

10. finishing something:

that wraps up our programme for this week; she bust up the marriage, not him; come on, drink up; they ate up and went

11. doing something thoroughly, or often just doing what an adjective implies:

she's in big trouble for bashing up the company car; you've fouled our plans up; should actors black up or not to play Othello?; it helps soften the material up; tighten this screw up; when the mixture has hardened up sufficiently

12. arriving somewhere, often in a negative sense:

we ended up in the pub of course; we're going to land up in hospital if you don't slow down

13. being confined:

he'll be locked up for several years; why don't you talk about your problems instead of bottling things up?; they've bricked the old doorway up

14. reducing something to smaller pieces:

chop the meat up for me; I hate the noise the waste disposal unit makes as it crunches everything up; slice it up into smaller pieces

15. producing something:

you owe me money, so fork up: he has been coughing up a lot of phlegm

UPON

sometimes interchangeable with 'on' (see ON) but often slightly more formal

WITH

1. in the home or presence of:

who did you stay with?; who did he come with?; their kids have nobody to play with

2. using something:

what was it painted with?; you can have the ones I've finished with

20 TYPES OF PHRASAL VERB

In the Phrasal Verb Dictionary in this book phrasal verbs have been classified as:

vi, vipo, vtsep, vtsep*, vtas, vtaspo.

VI (verb intransitive)

get off: he got off at Victoria Station

listen in: do you mind if I listen in while you talk?

VIPO (verb intransitive with prepositional object)

These are intransitive verbs combined with a particle which either can take or which must take an object:

join in: they all joined in the chorus (object 'chorus' can be omitted)

come across (find): where did you come across that word? (object 'word' necessary)

Especially in the second type, the combination behaves like a transitive verb and can often form a passive:

a type of virus which had never been come across before

VTSEP (verb transitive, separable)

The two parts of the verb may be separated:

dig up: they're digging the road up; they're digging up the road

A passive form is possible:

the road is being dug up again

If the object of the verb is a personal pronoun (or 'it') then the two parts of the verb MUST be separated:

look up: I'll look him up when I'm in Paris

VTSEP*

These are separable transitive verbs which can also take a form in which an object is used after the particle:

knock over: she knocked the coffee over (vtsep)

she knocked the coffee over the carpet (vtsep*)

(Note: adverbials such as '£10' in they've put the price up £10 have not been included in this classification; sometimes the * will apply, as shown, to only one category of a verb).

VTAS (verb transitive, always separate)

take back: the old song really took Grandpa back

The object CANNOT come after the particle

The passive is possible:

Grandpa was really taken back by the old song

VTASPO (verb transitive, always separate, with prepositional object)

The particle must always be separate from the verb AND an object MUST be used both after the verb and after the particle:

let in for: do you realize what you could be letting yourself in for?; he's let me in for a lot of extra work

PHRASAL VERB DICTIONARY

The following abbreviations have been used in this Phrasal Verb Dictionary:

Am	American English
Br	British English
Fam	familiar or informal or colloquial language
Fig	figurative
Sl	slang

Verb-type abbreviations are:

vi	verb intransitive
vipo	verb intransitive with a prepositional object
vtsep(*)	separable verb
vtas	verb that is always separate
vtaspo	verb that is always separate and that requires a prepositional object

For a full explanation of these categories see pages 92-93.

A

abide by *vipo* (*stick to*) you'll have to abide by the rules

account for *vipo* **(a)** (*explain*) how did they account for their absence?; there's no accounting for taste I suppose, but have you seen what they've done with their front room?; **(b)** (*count, establish whereabouts of*) the firemen did not need to enter the building since all the occupants were accounted for; **(c)** (*destroy*) in recent action, the rebels have accounted for a great many government troops; those two will account for as many sweets as all the other kids put together; **(d)** (*be source of*) shop-lifting accounts for most of the store's losses

act on (*or* **upon**) *vipo* **(a)** (*affect*) rust is caused by salt acting on metal; **(b)** (*respond to*) acting on her lawyer's advice, she has decided not to sue

act out *vtsep* (*make concrete*) he treats his patients for neuroses by having them act out their fantasies

act up *vi* (*misbehave*) that child acts up every time her mother goes out without her; the photocopier is acting up again

add in *vtsep** add in a little salt and the mixture is complete

add on *vtsep** (*attach*) we're thinking about adding on a conservatory; should we add something on as a tip?

add up **1** *vi* **(a)** (*with figures*) I'd have thought that at your age you could add up by now!; **(b)** (*make sense*) it's all beginning to add up; it's a mystery, it just doesn't add up; **2** *vtsep* if you add all the figures up the total is surprisingly large

add up to *vipo* **(a)** (*figures etc*) how much does it all add up to?; **(b)** (*amount to*) is that all you've done? – it doesn't add up to much, does it?; when you put all the facts together it adds up to quite an interesting case

adhere to *vipo* (*support*) I don't adhere to that philosophy at all

admit to *vipo* (*confess*) he admitted to a slight feeling of apprehension

agree on *vipo* (*reach agreement*) they cannot agree on a name for the baby; well, that's agreed on then

agree to *vipo* (*accept*) she felt she could not agree to my terms; they agreed to their son taking the job

agree with *vipo* **(a)** (*be of same opinion*) I am afraid I cannot agree with you; she doesn't agree with all this psychoanalytic treatment for child molesters; **(b)** (*suit*) seafood doesn't agree with me

allow for *vipo* (*take account of*) when calculating how much material you'll need, always allow for some wastage; I suppose I should allow for his inexperience; has that been allowed for in your figures?

allow out *vtsep* (*permit to go out*) the curfew meant that nobody was allowed out after dark; some prisoners are allowed out at weekends

angle for *vipo* (*try to obtain*) he was angling for promotion so he developed a sudden interest in the boss's daughter; never angle for compliments

answer back **1** *vi* **(a)** (*be impertinent*) don't answer back, young man!; **(b)** (*defend oneself*) she's the boss, so I can't answer back; **2** *vtsep* that child will answer anyone back

answer for *vipo* (*be responsible*) if he keeps on at me like this, I won't answer for my actions; the people who voted him in have a great deal to answer for

answer to *vipo* **(a)** (*be accountable to*) if you lay one finger on him you'll have me to answer to; who do you answer to in your job?; **(b)** (*correspond to*) a woman answering to the description has been seen in the area

argue away **1** *vtsep* (*make disappear*) you cannot argue the facts away – ozone depletion is a serious problem; **2** *vi* (*argue continuously*) they've been arguing away all morning

argue for/against *vipo* (*provide reasons for doing/not doing*) the speakers will argue for and against unilateral disarmament

argue out *vtsep* (*settle dispute*) I'll leave you to argue it out between you

ask after *vipo* (*send regards*) let your grandfather know I was asking after him

ask around **1** *vi* (*enquire*) I'll ask around at work and see if anyone else is interested; **2** *vtsep* (*invite*) why don't we ask them around for dinner one night

ask back *vtsep* (*invite*) do you want to ask them back for a drink after the theatre?

ask in *vtsep* (*invite*) I would ask you in for tea but my husband's not very well

ask out *vtsep* (*invite for a date etc*) he's asked her out so many times she must be running out of excuses by now; when he finally summoned up the courage to ask her out …

ask up *vtsep* (*invite*) don't get too excited if she asks you up for coffee – her mother lives with her!

attend to *vipo* **(a)** (*deal with*) are you being attended to, Madam?; I'll attend to this; **(b)** (*pay attention*) now attend to the experiment very closely, I'll be asking you questions later

auction off *vtsep* (*sell by auction*) they auctioned off all the family silver to raise some money

average out **1** *vtsep* (*calculate average*) I've averaged out how much I spend a week, and it's frightening; **2** *vi* (*amount to on average*) over a full year it averages out quite differently

average out at *vipo* (*amount to as an average*) how much does that average out at a year?

B

babble away/on *vi* (*talk incoherently*) you were babbling away in your sleep last night; I have no idea what you're babbling on about

back down *vi* (*give in*) he takes pride in never backing down, however strong the opposition's case

back on to *vipo* (*have at the rear*) the house backs on to a lane

back out **1** *vi* **(a)** (*leave backwards, especially in a car etc*) he backed out of the drive; **(b)** (*withdraw*) they can't back out from the deal now!; **2** *vtsep* (*remove backwards*) I'm not very good at backing the car out – will you do it?

back up **1** *vi* (*move backwards*) all the cars had to back up to let the ambulance past; **2** *vtsep* **(a)** (*support*) he'll need to back up his claim to the estate with something stronger than that; I doubt if the electors will back them up; **(b)** (*move backwards*) the driver had to back his lorry up all the way to the service station; **(c)** *Am* (*bring to stop*) the accident backed traffic up all the way to the turnpike

bail out *vtsep* **(a)** (*release from jail*) their lawyer bailed them out; **(b)** (*help*) I'm not bailing you out again – you're on your own this time

balance out 1 *vi* (*match*) the figures don't balance out; 2 *vtsep* (*match*) he cooks and she knows a lot about wine, so they balance each other out very nicely

bale out 1 *vi* **(a)** (*jump out of a plane*) Dad never tires of telling how he had to bale out over the Channel during a dogfight; **(b)** (*remove water from a boat*) she's taking on a lot of water – start baling out; 2 *vtsep* (*remove*) we'll have to bale the water out first

band together *vi* (*unite*) if we band together we can do something about this problem

bandy about/around *vtsep** (*use often, refers to words, names etc*) "decentralization" is a word the government bandies about a lot; the newspapers have been bandying that story around for weeks now

bank (up)on *vipo* (*rely*) him turn up on time? – I wouldn't bank on it if I were you

bargain for *vipo* (*expect*) if she marries him she'll get more than she bargained for; I didn't bargain for your kid brother coming as well

bash about *vtsep* Fam* (*beat, damage*) her husband bashes her about something awful; you can always rely on baggage handlers bashing your suitcases about

bash on *vi Sl* (*continue*) the weather forecast was bad but they decided to bash on with their plans for a picnic

battle on *vi* (*continue with difficulty*) he has fallen very far behind the leaders but he's still battling on; just battle on as best you can in the circumstances

bawl out *vtsep* **(a)** (*scream*) please don't bawl out my name; **(b)** (*scold*) the boss really bawled us out for that mistake

bear down 1 *vi* **(a)** (*push*) if that obstetrics nurse had said "bear down, dear" one more time, I would have screamed; **(b)** (*approach, especially in a threatening way*) the crew of the fishing boat jumped overboard as they saw the liner bearing down on them; the boys scattered as the headmaster bore down on them; **2** *vtsep* (*oppress*) the Third World is borne down by the burden of poverty

bear out *vtsep* (*support*) onlookers bore out her statement to the police; he feels that the report bears him out in his estimates of radiation levels in the area

bear up *vi* (*keep going*) Mother found it difficult to bear up when there was still no news after the second day; bear up! – just one more day to the weekend

bear (up)on *vipo* (*relate to*) I don't see how that bears on what I am supposed to be doing

bear with *vipo* (*be patient with*) the old lady asked the salesman to bear with her while she looked for her glasses

beat back *vtsep* (*repel, especially in battle*) they beat back the attackers three times but were eventually overrun

beat down **1** *vi* (*fall heavily*) the rain was beating down so fast it was difficult to see the road; **2** *vtsep* **(a)** (*make someone reduce a price*) I felt quite proud of myself for beating him down so much; **(b)** (*destroy*) the drunk threatened to beat the door down if they didn't open up; hailstorms have beaten down the county's entire barley crop

beat off *vtsep* (*repel*) the tourists tried unsuccessfully to beat off all the people trying to sell them things

beat out *vtsep* **(a)** (*extinguish*) desperate sheep-farmers were beating out the brush fires with their bare hands; **(b)** (*sound*) she beat out the rhythm on the table; **(c)** (*remove dent*) the door panel will have to be beaten out

beat up *vtsep* **(a)** (*attack*) beating up old ladies is his speciality; **(b)** (*mix*) just beat up a few eggs for an omelette

beaver away *vi Fam* (*work hard*) he's still beavering away at his studies

belt out *vtsep Fam* (*sing or play loudly*) he really belted that one out

belt up *vi* **(a)** *Sl* (*be silent*) I wish you would belt up; **(b)** (*fasten seat belt*) I'm not starting this car until you belt up

bind over *vtsep* (*give legal warning to*) he's the kind of judge who will bind people over rather than send them to prison; the drunk was bound over for three months to keep the peace

black out **1** *vi* (*lose consciousness*) she was alright until she saw the blood and then she blacked out; **2** *vtsep* **(a)** (*make dark*) the impact of the scene is heightened when they black the stage out; **(b)** (*prevent broadcast*) we regret that industrial action has blacked out this evening's programmes

blast off *vi* (*be launched*) the latest space shuttle blasted off at 5 am local time today

blaze away *vi* **(a)** (*shoot continuously*) the troops blazed away at the target; **(b)** (*burn*) the fire is blazing away merrily in the grate

blink at *vipo* (*deliberately ignore*) his wife blinks at his affairs

blink away *vtsep* (*make disappear*) I blinked my tears away

block in *vtsep* (*prevent from moving, usually cars*) that man next door has blocked me in again

block off *vtsep* (*close with barrier*) the street will be blocked off until the wreckage is cleared

block up *vtsep* **(a)** (*clog*) don't throw the tea leaves down the sink or you'll block it up; the worst thing about a cold is that your nose gets all blocked up; **(b)** (*close off*) they've blocked up the entry

blossom out *vi* (*become*) she's blossoming out into quite a beautiful young woman

blot out *vtsep* (*obliterate*) a word has been blotted out here; you must try to remember and come to terms with the past, not blot it out; the mist has blotted out the view

blow in **1** *vi* **(a)** (*be destroyed*) all the windows blew in because of the explosion; **(b)** (*come inside*) shut the door – the dust is blowing in; **(c)** *Fam* (*arrive suddenly*) when did you blow in?; **2** *vtsep* **(a)** (*destroy*) the blast blew all the windows in; **(b)** (*send in*) blow some more air in

blow off **1** *vi* (*disappear*) some of the roof tiles have blown off; **2** *vtsep* **(a)** (**make disappear, referring to wind etc*) the high winds blew the tiles off the roof; **(b)** (*with a gun, explosives*) the gunman threatened to blow their heads off

blow out **1** *vi* **(a)** (*be extinguished*) the candles have blown out; **(b)** (*explode*) the rear tyre blew out; **2** *vtsep* **(a)** (*extinguish*) be sure to blow the match out properly; the storm soon blew itself out; **(b)** (*set phrase*) (*kill*) to blow someone's brains out

blow over **1** *vi* **(a)** (*fall down*) the garage must have blown over in high winds last night; **(b)** (*come to an end, especially referring to arguments, bad moods etc*) it will soon blow over and you'll be friends again; the storm will blow over soon; **2** *vtsep* (*bring down*) did the wind blow anything over?

blow up 1 *vi* **(a)** (*explode*) the ammunitions depot blew up; **(b)** (*become angry*) do you often blow up like that?; **(c)** (*happen suddenly*) the argument blew up out of nowhere; **2** *vtsep* **(a)** (*destroy*) terrorists have blown up the presidential palace; **(b)** (*put air in*) do the tyres need blowing up?; **(c)** (*enlarge*) I'd like this photograph blown up; **(d)** (*exaggerate*) you're blowing this up out of all proportion

bluff out *vtsep* (*use cleverness to escape a difficult situation*) when the police get here we'll just have to bluff it out; she can bluff her way out of anything

board in/up *vtsep* (*barricade*) the windows and doors have all been boarded up to stop tramps getting in

bog down *vtsep usually passive* (*be stuck*) the car is bogged down in the mud; the important thing is not to get bogged down in details

boil down to *vi* (*amount to*) what his claim boils down to then is . . .

boil up **1** *vtsep* (*heat*) the doctor wants you to boil up some water; **2** *vi Fam* (*rise*) I could feel the anger boiling up inside me

bolt down **1** *vipo* (*descend quickly*) she bolted down the stairs and into the street; **2** *vtsep* (*eat quickly*) don't bolt your food down like that

bone up on *vipo Sl* (*study*) you'll have to bone up on your history if you want to pass that test next week

book in **1** *vi* (*register arrival at hotel*) do we have to book in by a certain time?; **2** *vtsep** (*make reservation for*) I've booked them into the best hotel in town

book out **1** *vi* (*register departure from hotel*) when do we have to book out by?; **2** *vtsep* (*register departure of*) the receptionist booked them out before noon

book up 1 *vi* (*make reservations*) have you booked up for a holiday?; 2 *vtsep usually passive* (*be full*) the hotel is all booked up

boot up 1 *vtsep* (*load, referring to computers*) use this diskette to boot the computer up; 2 *vi* (*load*) for some odd reason the computer is refusing to boot up

bottle up *vtsep* (*keep inside oneself*) it does no good to bottle your feelings up

bottom out *vi Fam* (*reach lowest point*) the government hopes that unemployment has finally bottomed out

bow out *vi Fam* (*leave, implying of one's own free will*) when the company brought in computers, old Mr Parsons decided the time had come to bow out

bowl out *vtsep* (*in cricket, eliminate*) we bowled him out for ten

bowl over *vtsep* **(a)** (*knock down*) the old lady was bowled over by a boy on a bike; **(b)** (*astonish*) I was bowled over by winning first prize

box in *vtsep* **(a)** (*surround*) the defence seem to have him boxed in; **(b)** (*enclose*) we're boxing in the sink; don't you feel boxed in in such a small room?

branch off *vi* (*diverge*) the road branches off to the left

branch out *vi* (*diversify*) the company intends to branch out into a new area of business

brazen out *vtsep* (*cope with a difficult situation by being insolent*) *usually 'to brazen it out'* when they accused him of gate-crashing the party, he brazened it out and refused to admit he hadn't been invited

break away *vi* **(a)** (*escape*) she broke away from the guards who were escorting her to hospital; **(b)** (*cut ties with*) when did you break away from your family?; it was the year France broke away from NATO; **(c)** (*crumble*) the merest touch and the surface breaks away

break down **1** *vi* **(a)** (*fail*) the car broke down on the motorway; that's where your argument breaks down; **(b)** (*collapse*) their marriage seems to be breaking down; talks between the two sides have broken down; I broke down in tears; **(c)** (*be able to be separated*) the compound breaks down into a number of components; **2** *vtsep* **(a)** (*destroy*) the firemen had to break down the door to rescue the children; **(b)** (*overcome*) she was unable to break down her parents' opposition to her plans; **(c)** (*separate into parts*) we really need to break the figures down a bit further

break in **1** *vi* **(a)** (*interrupt*) I really must break in at this point; **(b)** (*enter illegally*) when did you realize that someone had broken in?; **2** *vtsep* **(a)** (*destroy*) the thieves broke the door in; **(b)** (*train, accustom to being used*) she's good at breaking in horses; I hate having to break new shoes in

break into *vipo* **(a)** (*burgle*) thieves broke into a number of houses on the street last night; **(b)** (*use part of*) I'll have to break into my holiday money to pay for the repairs to my car; **(c)** (*interrupt*) why did you break into the conversation like that?; **(d)** (*start suddenly*) I broke into a cold sweat when I realized how high up I was; he often breaks into song in the shower

break off **1** *vi* **(a)** (*become detached*) it just broke off in my hand, honestly; **(b)** (*stop*) can we break off for the rest of the day?; **(c)** (*stop speaking*) he broke off when the chairman entered the room; **2** *vtsep* **(a)** (**remove*) break off two pieces of chocolate for you and your brother; **(b)** (*end*) talks have been broken off; **(c)** (*end relationship or engagement*) it wouldn't surprise me if they broke it off soon; I've broken it off with him

break out *vi* **(a)** (*suddenly begin*) fires have broken out all over the city; **(b)** (*develop*) the baby is breaking out into a rash; **(c)** (*escape*) the prisoners broke out late last night; **(d)** (*suddenly say*) "I don't agree", she broke out; **(e)** (*open, usually wine*) let's break out another bottle

break up **1** *vi* **(a)** (*disintegrate*) the ice on the river is breaking up at last; their marriage is breaking up; I just broke up (*with laughter*) at that joke; **(b)** (*end*) when did the party finally break up?; the schools will be breaking up for summer soon; **(c)** (*end relationship*) I've heard that they're breaking up; **2** *vtsep* **(a)** (*reduce to components*) you'll have to break the earth up before you can plant anything; **(b)** (*bring to end*) the warder broke up the fight between the prisoners; it was his drinking that broke the marriage up

bring about *vtsep* (*cause*) what brought this about?

bring back *vtsep* **(a)** (*lead*) Mum told me to bring you back for supper; **(b)** (*restore*) a couple of days in bed will bring him back to normal; it will be up to the electors to decide whether to bring back the previous government; **(c)** (*cause to return*) that song brings back memories

bring down *vtsep* **(a)** (*destroy*) if that boy doesn't stop jumping up and down like that he's going to bring the house down about our ears; (*set phrase*) their jokes always bring the house down (*ie receive a lot of laughter in a theatre etc*); **(b)** (*shoot down*) the spy plane was brought down by a missile; **(c)** (*land*) the badly damaged plane was brought down with no loss of life; **(d)** (*cause* *to fall*) it was really the students who brought down the government; that tackle brought him down; **(e)** (*cause to appear, referring especially to a person in authority etc*) stop making so much noise or you'll bring the headmaster down on us; **(f)** (*reduce*) this new drug will bring his temperature down; she would have brought the price down even further if you'd gone on bargaining

bring in *vtsep* **(a)** (*lead*) I've brought Mrs Jones in to see you; **(b)** (*introduce*) new tax legislation will be brought in next year; **(c)** (*involve*) the company is bringing consultants in to see if the problems can be solved; this argument is between you two – why bring me in?; **(d)** (*set phrase*) to bring in the New Year (*ie celebrate it*); **(e)** (*earn*) how much money is your eldest son bringing in?; **(f)** (*reach*) the jury brought in a verdict of not guilty

bring off *vtsep* **(a)** (**remove*) the bodies are being brought off the ship today; **(b)** (*complete successfully*) did you bring the deal off?

bring on *vtsep* **(a)** (*introduce*) please bring on our next contestant; **(b)** (*cause to appear*) damp days always bring on my arthritis; what brought this on?; **(c)** (*help develop*) this mild weather will bring the roses on nicely; **(d)** (*set phrase*) I brought it on myself I suppose (*ie it was my own fault*)

bring out *vtsep* **(a)** (*lead*) they brought the man out under armed guard; **(b)** (*make less shy*) his grand-daughter is about the only one who can bring him out (of himself); **(c)** (*cause to appear*) the sun has brought out all the bulbs; disasters bring out the best – and worst – in people; they're bringing out the new models very soon; strawberries bring her out in a rash

bring round *vtsep* **(a)** (*lead*) I'll bring him round to meet you some time; **(b)** (*persuade*) you'll never bring my dad round to that way of thinking; **(c)** (*restore to consciousness*) they brought her round quite quickly after she fainted; **(d)** (*steer*) I finally managed to bring the conversation round to what I wanted to talk about

bring up *vtsep* **(a)** (*rear*) we've brought four kids up; **(b)** (*mention*) Madam Chairwoman, I wish to bring up the question of travel expenses; **(c)** (*vomit*) everything she swallows she brings up ten minutes later

brown off *vtsep Fam* (*annoy*) I'm browned off with always having to do the dishes; he's very browned off with you because you didn't go to the party; you're all looking a bit browned off – what's wrong?

brush aside *vtsep* (*reject, not deal with*) the Minister brushed aside the reporters; she won't listen – just brushes our objections aside

brush up *vtsep* **(a)** (*collect with brush*) I want all those crumbs brushed up off the floor; **(b)** (*improve*) he'll have to brush up his Spanish

buck up **1** *vi* **(a)** (*hurry*) buck up or we'll be late; **(b)** (*be cheerful*) I wish he would buck up a little; **2** *vtsep* **(a)** (*make cheerful*) the good news bucked me up no end; **(b)** (*set phrase*) to buck up one's ideas (*ie be more efficient, honest, regular etc, change for the better*)

bucket down *vi Fam* (*rain heavily*) it's bucketing down

buckle down/to *vi* (*set to work*) I suppose I had better buckle down if I want to finish the housework this morning; if you don't buckle down to your piano practice . . .; he buckled to and finished cleaning the car

build on **1** *vtsep** (*add to existing structure*) next door are building on a conservatory; **2** *vipo* (*use as a foundation*) the company is building on its earlier success

build up **1** *vi* (*increase*) pressure on the government is building up; **2** *vtsep* **(a)** (*increase*) I wouldn't build my hopes up if I were you; we're trying to build up our savings so we can buy a house soon; **(b)** (*create*) his father built that company up from nothing; you've built up quite a reputation for yourself; **(c)** (*strengthen*) the children need some vitamins to build them up; **(d)** *usually passive* (*cover with houses*) the area has become quite built up; **(e)** (*publicize*) the play has been so built up that it's impossible to get tickets for it

bump into *vipo* **(a)** (*collide with*) I was so engrossed in my thoughts that I bumped into a lamp post; **(b)** (*meet*) he's always bumping into people he knows

bump off *vtsep Sl* (*kill*) his job was bumping people off for a fee

bump up *vtsep Fam* (*increase*) they've bumped up the price of beer again

bundle off *vtsep** (*send hastily*) the baby was bundled off to hospital in an ambulance

bung up *vtsep Fam* (*block*) who bunged the sink up?; I'm/my nose is all bunged up

burn down **1** *vi* (*be destroyed by fire*) the theatre burned down; (*become less intense*) the fire is burning down; **2** *vtsep* vandals have burned down a number of derelict buildings in the area

burn out **1** *vi* (*lose heat*) the fire is burning out; *Fig* social workers frequently burn out at an early age; **2** *vtsep* **(a)** (*make homeless by fire*) they were burned out; **(b)** (*come to an end*) the fire has burnt itself out

burn up 1 *vi* (*be consumed*) the rocket burned up in the atmosphere; **2** *vtsep* (*consume*) children burn up a lot of energy playing; this stove burns up a lot of wood

burst into *vipo* **(a)** (*enter noisily*) she burst into the room; **(b)** (*suddenly start*) he burst into tears; then they all burst into song

burst out *vi* **(a)** (*do/say suddenly*) I burst out laughing; "where were you last night?", he burst out; **(b)** (*leave noisily*) they all burst out of the room

butt in *vi* (*interfere*) we were just having a cosy chat when she butted in; is this a private argument or can anybody butt in?

buy into *vipo* (*purchase share in*) he has bought into his neighbour's business

buy off *vtsep Fam* (*bribe*) the councillor was bought off with an all-expenses paid holiday in the south of France

buy out *vtsep* (*purchase shares of*) all the other shareholders have been bought out

buy up *vtsep* (*purchase*) look at all those parcels – she must have bought up the entire store!

buzz off *vi Fam* (*go away*) tell that kid brother of yours to buzz off; just buzz off and leave me alone

C

call back 1 *vi* **(a)** (*return*) I'll call back later to see her; **(b)** (*telephone again*) if you'd like to call back in an hour . . .; **2** *vtsep* **(a)** (*telephone again*) he said he would call you back; **(b)** (*summon again*) I know she's on holiday but she'll have to be called back to deal with this; I think the last pair should be called back for another audition

call for *vipo* **(a)** (*request*) the Opposition is calling for her resignation; **(b)** (*collect*) would it be too much of a rush if I called for you at seven?; **(c)** (*require*) this is the kind of job that calls for brains rather than brawn; that's wonderful news – it calls for a celebration

call in 1 *vi* **(a)** (*visit*) the social worker is going to call in later; **(b)** (*report by telephone*) off-duty nurses called in and offered to help; prison officers are not actually on strike but a great many of them are calling in sick; **2** *vtsep* **(a)** (*summon*) they've finally decided to call the doctor in; **(b)** (*summon return of*) the bank has called in its loans

call off *vtsep* **(a)** (*cancel*) the meeting will have to be called off; does this mean we'll have to call our holiday off?; they've called it off (*ie engagement or wedding*); **(b)** (**tell to come away*) call your dog off!

call out 1 *vi* (*shout*) don't call out in the street like that; **2** *vtsep* **(a)** (*shout*) the master of ceremonies called out the names of the prizewinners; **(b)** (*summon*) call out the guard!; I don't like calling the doctor out at this time of night; **(c)** (*order to strike*) the men were called out halfway through the morning shift

call up *vtsep* **(a)** (*summon*) the situation looked dangerous and the lieutenant decided to call up reinforcements; **(b)** (*summon to join army*) Dad was called up in 1940; **(c)** (*telephone to*) please don't call me up at midnight; **(d)** (*evoke*) the speech called up thoughts of the past

call (up) on *vipo* **(a)** (*visit*) gentlemen used to ask permission to call on young ladies; **(b)** (*exhort*) the opposition called on the government to make its position clear

calm down 1 *vi* (*become quiet*) getting hysterical won't help, just calm down; I want you all to calm down now, children; **2** *vtsep* (*sooth*) leave it to Mum, she'll calm him down

care for *vipo* **(a)** (*tend*) she has spent years caring for her invalid mother; **(b)** (*like*) you know I don't care for that kind of language; I don't believe he ever cared for you or he wouldn't have treated you the way he did

carry away *vtsep* (*make excited, over-enthusiastic*) he let his enthusiasm carry him away; she gets carried away by the sound of her own voice; take it easy, don't get carried away!

carry forward *vtsep* **(a)** (*put to a later date*) can I carry my leave forward and have six weeks next summer?; **(b)** (*in accounting*) this amount should have been carried forward to the next page

carry off *vtsep* **(a)** (*capture*) she carried off the prizes for Latin and French; **(b)** (*manage*) it wasn't the easiest of speeches to make but you carried it off very well; **(c)** (*kill, referring to diseases*) tuberculosis carried off a great many people in the last century

carry on **1** *vi* **(a)** (*continue*) just carry on with what you were doing; **(b)** *Fam* (*make a scene, behave badly*) he carried on just because his wife wanted an evening out; what a way to carry on!; **(c)** (*have an affair*) have you been carrying on behind my back?; **2** *vtsep* (*continue*) grandfather wants me to carry on the business after he dies; we have carried on a correspondence for years

carry out *vtsep* **(a)** (*remove in arms*) they had to carry him out since he couldn't walk; **(b)** (*do, execute*) never make a promise that you cannot carry out; the coast guard is carrying out a search for the missing crew members

carry through *vtsep* (*execute*) the plan has to be carried through to the last detail

carve out *vtsep* **(a)** (*make from wood or stone*) he has now carved out twenty or so statues; **(b)** (*develop*) the company plans to carve out its own niche on the market

carve up *vtsep* **(a)** (*cut*) ask the butcher to carve the meat up for you; **(b)** (*divide*) they just carved up the land among themselves with no regard for the native inhabitants; **(c)** *Fam* (*overtake dangerously on road*) did you see how that fool carved me up?

cash in **1** *vtsep* (*exchange for money*) are you going to cash in your premium bonds?; **2** *vipo* (*derive benefit from*) she's cashing in on the fact that her father knows a lot of influential people

cast away *vtsep* (*abandon*) Robinson Crusoe was cast away on his desert island for a great many years

cast back *vtsep* (*direct backwards*) if you cast your mind back a week, you will recall that . . .

cast off **1** *vtsep* **(a)** (*end knitting*) cast off the remaining stitches; **(b)** (*release from mooring*) we cast the launch off at dawn; **2** *vi* **(a)** (*end knitting*) cast off when only four stitches remain; **(b)** (*release boat from mooring*) they will cast off shortly

cast on **1** *vi* (*start knitting*) I usually cast on with my thumb; **2** *vtsep* (*make stitches*) cast on 80 stitches; have you cast the sleeve on yet?

catch at *vipo* (*grab at*) she caught at his sleeve and asked for help

catch on *vi* **(a)** (*become popular*) I remember you saying that the Beatles would never catch on; **(b)** *Fam* (*understand*) she's so naive she didn't catch on

catch out *vtsep* **(a)** (*trap*) the police caught him out by asking for a description of the programme he said he was watching; **(b)** (*in cricket, eliminate*) he was caught out very early on

catch up 1 *vi* (*close gap, get closer*) the runners behind are catching up; I wish I could catch up with my work/sleep; **2** *vtsep* **(a)** (*overtake*) you go ahead and I'll catch you up; **(b)** (*become entangled*) they were caught up in a traffic jam for hours

cave in *vi* (*collapse*) the walls and roof caved in under the force of the blast

centre on *vipo* (*concentrate on*) the play centres on the idea of survivor guilt

chain up *vtsep* (*secure*) I hope he chains that brute of a dog up at night; people could be chained up in prison for years

chalk up *vtsep Fam* **(a)** (*achieve*) the team chalked up another win today; **(b)** (*give credit in a shop etc*) chalk it up, will you, and I'll pay next week; **(c)** (*register as*) she'll just have to chalk it up to experience (*ie simply regard it as one of life's experiences*)

chance on *vipo* (*find by accident*) I chanced on this piece of Meissen in a grubby little second-hand shop

change down *vi* (*use lower gear in car*) traffic lights coming up – change down

change over *vi* **(a)** (*convert*) is it a good idea to change over entirely to electricity?; **(b)** (*switch*) let's change over and you wash while I dry; as soon as opera or ballet comes on the TV, he changes over (*ie to another programme*)

change up *vi* (*use higher gear*) you have to change up faster than that

chase up *vtsep* (*locate, implying that something/someone is difficult to find*) why not ask one of the big stores to chase up the pattern for you?; we finally chased her up in the library

chat up *vtsep Fam* (*talk flirtatiously to someone of the* *opposite sex*) he's just chatting you up; I wish I could chat up men the way she does

cheat on *vipo* **(a)** (*be unfaithful to in sexual matters*) why didn't you tell me he was cheating on me?; **(b)** (*be dishonest about*) it's not a good idea to cheat on your expenses

check in **1** *vi* (*register arrival at hotel*) have you checked in?; **2** *vtsep* **(a)** (*register arrival of*) they must be here – I checked them in myself; **(b)** (*make reservation for*) she's quite high-powered, so check her into a four-star hotel

check out **1** *vi* **(a)** (*leave hotel*) they checked out last night; **(b)** *Sl* (*make sense*) it doesn't check out; **2** *vtsep* (*investigate*) we've checked her out and she's who she says she is; **(b)** (*register departure of*) the reception clerk will check you out

check through *vtsep* **(a)** (*examine*) they checked through everyone's hand luggage; **(b)** (*send by plane*) I have to change at Geneva – can my bags be checked right through to London?

cheer on *vtsep* (*support*) he's there every Saturday to cheer his team on

cheer up **1** *vi* (*become cheerful*) I hate it when people tell you to cheer up; **2** *vtsep* **(a)** (*make cheerful*) a visit to the pub will cheer him up; **(b)** (*make bright*) the new curtains really do cheer the room up

chew on *vipo* **(a)** (*gnaw*) he chewed on his pipe stem for a bit and then said . . .; **(b)** (*think about with a view to making a decision*) how much longer do you need to chew on it?

chew over *vtsep* (*think about with a view to reaching a decision*) I have been chewing this little problem over in my mind, Watson, and . . .

chew up *vtsep* **(a)** (*use teeth to chew thoroughly*) chew your food up well before swallowing; **(b)** (*destroy*) your machine has chewed up my bank card; it's those heavy lorries that are chewing up the road

chicken out *vi Fam* (*refuse through nervousness*) I arranged a blind date with Annabel for my brother but he chickened out at the last minute; don't chicken out on us; he chickened out of his dental appointment

chip in *Fam* **1** *vi* **(a)** (*interrupt*) if I can chip in for a moment . . .; **(b)** (*contribute*) we've all chipped in for a present for her; **2** *vtsep* (*contribute*) how much is everyone else chipping in?

chip off **1** *vi* (*fall*) the paint is chipping off; **2** *vtsep** (*remove*) be careful with those plates – I don't want any pieces chipped off

choke back *vtsep* (*suppress*) looking at these pictures, I find it hard to choke back my tears/anger

choke up *vtsep* (*clog*) the drain is all choked up with leaves

chuck in/up *vtsep Fam* (*abandon*) you're surely not thinking of chucking up your job?; one day I'm going to chuck all this in and buy a farm; he's chucked his latest girlfriend in

chug along *vi Fam* (*move slowly*) Dad always chugs along at about 35, even on the motorway

clam up *vi* (*refuse to talk*) don't clam up on me, talk to me!

clamp down *vi* (*become stricter*) the police are clamping down this Christmas so don't drink and drive

clamp down on *vipo* (*become stricter about*) the authorities are clamping down on misleading advertising

clean out *vtsep* **(a)** (*make tidy*) I'll clean out a few cupboards today I think; **(b)** *Fam* (*leave without money*) the casino cleaned him out; **(c)** *Fam* (*buy/take all of*) someone has cleaned the shop out of sugar

clean up 1 *vtsep* (a) (*remove dirt*) when are you going to clean this place up – it's a mess; the kids need to be cleaned up before we go to your mother's; (b) (*remove bad elements from*) I like those old cowboy films where the sheriff always says "I'm going to clean up this town"; 2 *vi Fam* (*make money*) she really cleaned up at the roulette table

clear away 1 *vtsep* (*remove*) workmen were clearing away the debris; it's your turn to clear the dishes away; 2 *vi* (*disappear*) the clouds have all cleared away

clear off 1 *vtsep** (*remove*) clear all those papers off the table; 2 *vi* (*go away*) clear off!; the boys cleared off when they saw the headmaster coming down the street

clear up 1 *vtsep* (a) (*settle, clarify*) I'd like to clear up a point or two; we have some problems that need to be cleared up; (b) (*tidy*) I can't come out – I have to clear up my room; (c) (*cure*) the doctor said this cream would clear up the acne; 2 *vi* (a) (*become fine, referring to the weather*) it's clearing up; (b) (*disappear*) don't worry – that rash will soon clear up

climb down *vi* (a) (*descend*) it took the climbers three hours to climb down; (b) (*admit error*) she'll never climb down, however strong the arguments against her

clock in 1 *vi* (a) (*have a time of*) the last of the marathon runners clocked in at six hours; (b) (*record arrival at work*) I have to clock in; you clocked in 10 minutes late; 2 *vtsep* (*record someone else's arrival*) do you think just this once you could clock me in?

clock off 1 *vi* (*finish work by marking a time card*) when did you clock off?; 2 *vtsep* I'll clock you off if you like

clock up *vtsep* (a) (*achieve in a race*) he clocked up a faster time than any of his rivals in the race; (b) *Fam* (*achieve, win*) the team has clocked up another victory

close down 1 *vi* (a) (*shut permanently*) the factory is closing down next month; we're closing down soon; (b) (*end*) television closes down a lot later than it used to; 2 *vtsep* (*shut permanently*) they closed the restaurant down because of health code violations

close in 1 *vi* (a) (*become shorter*) the days are closing in; (b) (*approach, often in a threatening way*) winter is closing in; government troops are said to be closing in on the rebels; 2 *vtsep* (*enclose*) they're thinking of closing the porch in

close up 1 *vi* (*come closer together*) the photographer asked the people in the front line to close up so he could get them all in; 2 *vtsep* (*seal*) they must have gone away for some time – the house is all closed up; the opening in the fence has been closed up to prevent similar tragedies in the future

cloud up 1 *vi* (*become cloudy*) it's clouding up; the mirror has clouded up; 2 *vtsep* (*make cloudy*) the bathroom is poorly ventilated – steam always clouds the windows up

club together *vi* (*pool money*) if we club together, we can get one big present instead of lots of small ones

cobble together *vtsep* (*do hastily*) my speech won't be very good I'm afraid – I cobbled it together on the train

collect up *vtsep* (*gather*) I began to collect up my parcels

comb through *vipo* (*search thoroughly*) I've combed through the entire book and haven't found any reference to him

come across **1** *vi* (*make an impression*) how did her story come across?; they come across as (being) rather nice people; **2** *vipo* (*find*) I came across this when I was tidying up – is it yours?

come across with *vipo Fam* (*supply*) if we don't come across with the money, they say they'll kill him

come along *vi* **(a)** (*hurry*) come along children, please!; **(b)** (*make progress*) my speech was coming along rather well until yesterday; **(c)** (*arrive*) everything was peaceful until you came along

come apart *vi* (*fall to pieces*) honestly, I don't know how it happened – it just came apart in my hands; she feels her life is coming apart at the seams

come at *vipo* (*attack*) the pair of them came at me with a baseball bat

come away *vi* **(a)** (*leave*) why not come away with me to Paris for the weekend?; come away from that cat – it's got fleas; **(b)** (*become detached*) the handle has come away from the knife

come back *vi* **(a)** (*return to memory*) I've forgotten your name but it will come back eventually; **(b)** (*make progress after being in a losing position, return*) we thought it was all over but he's coming back very strongly now; **(c)** (*retort*) then she came back with one of her usual cutting remarks

come by **1** *vipo* (*acquire*) how did your brother come by all those bruises?; **2** *vi* (*visit*) I'll come by next week if that suits

come down *vi* **(a)** (*decrease*) oil prices have been coming down; her temperature came down overnight; **(b)** (*reduce prices*) he'll come down a few pounds if you bargain; **(c)** (*be removed*) that disgusting poster is coming down right now – or else; **(d)** (*be reduced in status*) this is what we've come down to – selling the family silver; **(e)** (*be a question of*) it all comes down to money; **(f)** (*reach*) the curtains should come right down to the floor; **(g)** (*be an inheritance*) the necklace came down to her from her great-aunt

come down on *vipo* **(a)** (*criticize, punish*) one mistake and he'll come down on you like a ton of bricks; **(b)** (*decide in favour of*) he'll wait and see what happens and then come down on the winning side

come down with *vipo* (*succumb to, referring to diseases*) I always come down with a cold at this time of year

come forward *vi* (*present oneself*) the police have appealed for witnesses to come forward

come in *vi* **(a)** (*arrive*) our new stock will not come in until next week; **(b)** (*receive money*) I don't have much coming in at the moment – can you wait a bit?; **(c)** (*have a role*) where does she come in in all this?; an extra pair of hands always comes in useful; **(d)** (*contact by radio*) are you receiving me? come in, please

come in for *vipo* (*receive*) the government is coming in for a lot of criticism over its latest proposals; he came in for a lot of adverse publicity when he was younger

come in on *vipo* (*be given a part in*) why should we let him come in on the deal?

come into *vipo* **(a)** (*inherit*) she'll come into a tidy little sum when her great-uncle dies; **(b)** (*be involved in*) wait a minute – when did I come into this crazy scheme?; ability doesn't come into it – it's who you know that matters; **(c)** (*set phrases*) my cherry tree has come into blossom early this year; when does the poll tax come into effect?; would you mind explaining how the car came into your possession, sir?

come of *vipo* **(a)** (*result from*) nothing will come of it; this is what comes of being too cocky; **(b)** (*derive from*) the mare comes of good stock; **(c)** (*set phrase*) she inherited a fortune when she came of age (*ie reached legal adult status*)

come off **1** *vi* **(a)** (*become detached*) could you fix my bike? – the chain has come off; I'm afraid the carpet is ruined – wine stains never come off; **(b)** (*take place*) I shall be very surprised if that wedding ever comes off; **(c)** (*succeed*) yet another attempt to beat the record that hasn't come off; **(d)** (*escape*) considering what he's done, he has come off very lightly; it could have been a serious accident, but they all came off without a scratch; **(e)** (*acquit oneself*) we came off very badly in the debate on capital punishment; **(f)** *Sl* (*have orgasm*) he did eventually come off but it was a long wait; **2** *vipo* **(a)** (*be removed from*) that kind of mark never comes off silk; **(b)** (*become detached from*) the handle has come off the knife; they're threatening to come off the gold standard; **(c)** (*exclamation of impatience, disbelief*) come off it – I've heard that line before

come on *vi* **(a)** (*hurry*) come on, or we'll miss the start; **(b)** (*make progress*) how's the work coming on?; **(c)** (*start*) the rain came on about six; I have a sore throat coming on; when does that programme you want to watch come on?; **(d)** (*appear*) the character he plays doesn't come on until halfway through the first act; **(e)** *Sl* (*give impression of being*) she tried to come on like a femme fatale but soon gave it up; he was coming on a bit too macho

come out *vi* **(a)** (*appear*) the magazine comes out on a Wednesday; when do you expect your latest film to come out?; now that the sun has come out maybe I'll get my washing dried; next door's roses always come out early; **(b)** (*become known*) the election results came out a few hours ago; the truth will come out eventually; **(c)** (*go on strike*) nurses all over the country have come out in protest; **(d)** (*develop*) the baby has come out in a rash; **(e)** (*be successful, referring to photographs*) they're pleased that their holiday photographs have come out so well; **(f)** (*disappear*) I've had this coat cleaned three times and the stain still hasn't come out; **(g)** (*leave hospital, prison*) she'll be coming out soon; **(h)** (*be solved*) of course the equation hasn't come out – you copied the figures down wrongly; **(i)** (*decide*) we've come out against the idea of moving; the committee came out in her favour; **(j)** (*emerge, from situation*) she came out of that looking rather silly, don't you think?

come out with *vipo* (*say, usually referring to something unexpected*) I'm always on the edge of my seat wondering what he'll come out with next; she finally came out with what was bothering her

come over **1** *vi* **(a)** (*change allegiance*) I doubt if I will ever come over to your way of thinking; **(b)** (*make impression*) he comes over as (being) a bit pompous, but in fact he's rather shy; **(c)** (*suddenly become, referring to feelings, moods etc*) Granny says she came over all funny in the supermarket; **2** *vipo* (*happen to, referring to moods etc*) I don't know what's come over her – she's usually such a quiet little thing

come round *vi* **(a)** (*become amenable*) give him time – he'll come round eventually; I'm sure they'll come round to our point of view in the end; **(b)** (*regain consciousness*) imagine that poor woman coming round and seeing all those faces staring at her; **(c)** (*recur*) he swears birthdays come round more often after you're 40

come through **1** *vi* **(a)** (*arrive*) he's champing at the bit because his visa is taking so long to come through; **(b)** (*survive*) it must have been a terrifying experience but they have come through all right; **2** *vipo* **(a)** (*succeed*) their daughter has come through her law exams with flying colours; **(b)** (*survive*) I am sure you will come through this ordeal; very few people came through the First World War unscarred either physically or mentally

come to **1** *vi* (*regain consciousness*) she came to in a hospital bed; **2** *vipo* **(a)** (*amount to*) the bill came to much more than I could afford; that nephew of his will never come to anything; has it come to this, that we must leave a house our family has lived in for 400 years?; **(b)** (*be a question of*) when it comes to buying a car, find yourself a reputable dealer; **(c)** (*get as far as*) if it comes to a malpractice suit, the surgeon is in trouble; when does the case come to trial?; I do wish she would come to the point; **(d)** (*set phrases*) come to that, where were you last night?; it's really come to something when old age pensioners have to live off dog food

come up *vi* (*appear*) when does her case come up (for trial)?; he beat a hasty retreat when the subject of fee-paying schools came up; do you think this question will come up in the exam?; two other houses in our street are coming up for sale soon; my number never comes up in the draw; the bulbs are starting to come up; call me if anything comes up that you can't handle

come up against *vipo* (*encounter*) you realize that you'll come up against some pretty strong opposition on this?; who does she come up against in the next round?

come up to *vipo* **(a)** (*reach*) she's so tall that I only come up to her shoulder; we're coming up to the halfway mark now; **(b)** (*equal*) his latest play does not come up to expectations

come up with *vipo* (*produce unexpectedly*) she's come up with a solution; he keeps coming up with these awful jokes; I'll let you know if I come up with anything that might help

conk out *vi Sl* **(a)** (*lose consciousness*) he's conked out – better send for a doctor; **(b)** (*stop working*) the radio has conked out on us

cool down **1** *vi* **(a)** (*become calm*) we'll talk about it once you've cooled down; **(b)** (*become cool*) it has cooled down quite a bit since yesterday; things have cooled down between them; **2** *vtsep* **(a)** (*make calm*) I'll try to cool her down but I don't think I'll have much success; **(b)** (*make cool*) how about a beer to cool you down after all that hard work?

cotton on *vi Fam* (*understand, realize*) I never did cotton on

cough up **1** *vtsep* **(a)** (*produce by coughing*) if you can cough the phlegm up, you'll soon feel better; people with tuberculosis cough up blood; **(b)** *Fam* (*pay*) I've got to cough up another £50; **2** *vi Fam* (*pay*) he coughed up for the meal

count in *vtsep* (*include*) have you counted the neighbours in?; anybody want to go out for lunch? – count me in!

count on *vipo* (*depend on*) we can always count on you to be late; he counted on me and I let him down

count out *vtsep* **(a)** (*calculate*) if you want to know how much money you have, count it out; **(b)** (*in* *boxing*) his opponent is on the canvas and being counted out; **(c)** (*exclude*) he's teetotal, so count him out of the pub crawl; a weekend camping out in the snow? – no thanks, count me out!

count up *vtsep* (*calculate*) I've counted these figures up time and time again and get a different answer every time

cover up **1** *vi* (*conceal something*) don't try to cover up – I know it was you; the architects and builders are covering up for each other; the government was accused of covering up; **2** *vtsep* **(a)** (*put cover on*) that dress is much too low – cover yourself up a bit; **(b)** (*conceal*) it's highly unlikely that he meant to cover things up

crack down *vi* (*be stricter*) in view of the increase in drunk driving the police are going to crack down

crack down on *vipo* (*be stricter with*) they're going to crack down on drunk drivers

crack up *vi* **1 (a)** (*break*) the ice on the pond is cracking up; **(b)** (*collapse*) if he doesn't take a holiday soon, he'll crack up; do you think their marriage is cracking up?; she cracked up under the pressure; **(c)** (*be helpless with laughter*) I cracked up when he said that; **2** *vtsep Fam* (*praise, claim to be*) foreign holidays are not what they're cracked up to be

cream off *vtsep* (*remove, take for oneself, referring to the best*) the oldest universities cream off the best candidates

cross off *vtsep** (*remove*) cross his name off the list

cross out *vtsep* (*draw line through*) cross your mistakes out neatly, please

cry off *vi* (*cancel acceptance of invitation*) I hate it when people cry off at the last minute

cry out *vi* **(a)** (*shout*) the pain made her cry out; **(b)** (*need desperately*) that room is just crying out for red velvet curtains

cuddle up *vi* (*lie closely*) cuddle up if you're cold; the little girl cuddled up to her grandmother

curl up *vi* **(a)** (*lie comfortably*) I like to curl up in bed with a good book; **(b)** (*form a curl*) hedgehogs curl up into a ball for protection

cut across *vipo* **(a)** (*take shorter way*) we cut across the playing field; **(b)** (*go across limits of*) concern for the environment cuts across party lines

cut back **1** *vi* (*reduce spending*) we're definitely going to have to cut back; **2** *vtsep* (*prune*) now is the time to cut your raspberries back; the company is cutting back production until the seamen's strike is over

cut down **1** *vtsep* **(a)** (*fell*) they're cutting down the trees that were damaged in the storm; **(b)** (*kill*) he was cut down by machine-gun fire; **2** *vi* (*reduce consumption*) if you won't stop smoking then at least cut down

cut in **1** *vi* **(a)** (*interrupt*) the interviewer cut in to ask a question; **(b)** (*swerve*) that idiot will cause an accident cutting in in front of people like that; **2** *vtsep* (*include in*) can you cut me in on one of your deals?

cut off **1** *vtsep* **(a)** (**remove by cutting*) they had to cut his clothes off in the emergency room; cut off his head!; **(b)** (*isolate*) the town has been cut off by floods; don't you feel cut off living in the country?; **(c)** (*disconnect, referring especially to telephone, electricity etc*) we'd hardly said hello before we were cut off; it's dreadful to think how many people have their electricity cut off because they can't afford to pay the bills; **(d)** (*disinherit*) the old man cut his son off without the proverbial penny

cut out 1 *vi* (*stop*) will you have a look at the engine – it keeps cutting out; **2** *vtsep* **(a)** (*remove by cutting*) I cut this magazine article out for you; **(b)** (*shape by cutting*) the worst bit is cutting the dress out; **(c)** (*eliminate*) cut out starchy food for a couple of weeks; **(d)** *Fam* (*stop*) I've told you already to cut out the silly jokes; **(e)** *Fig usually passive* (*be suited*) I'm not cut out for all these late nights

cut up *vtsep* **(a)** (*chop*) cut the meat up quite small; **(b)** *usually passive* (*upset*) he was definitely a bit cut up about not being invited

D

dash off **1** *vi* (*leave hurriedly*) she was sorry she missed you but she had to dash off; **2** *vtsep* (*write/paint quickly*) I dashed off an answer yesterday; he says he dashes these paintings off in his spare time

deal with *vipo* **(a)** (*do business with*) armament manufacturers will deal with anybody; **(b)** (*handle*) she dealt with that problem very well; the case wasn't very professionally dealt with; **(c)** (*be about*) the play deals with euthanasia

die away *vi* (*fade*) the noise of the car engine died away

die down *vi* (*subside*) he had to wait for the applause to die down

die off *vi* (*die one by one*) by the time he was in his twenties, his relatives had all died off; their livestock is dying off as the drought intensifies

die out *vi* (*become extinct*) entire species are dying out as their habitat is being destroyed

dig in **1** *vi* **(a)** (*make trenches*) the first thing the troops had to do when they got to the front was to dig in; (**b**) *Fam* (*start to eat*) dig in – there's lots more where that came from; **2** *vtsep* (*add by digging*) before planting, dig in a couple of handfuls of bone meal

dig into *vipo* (**a**) *Fam* (*eat heartily*) dig into that pie as much as you like – I made two; (**b**) (*investigate*) they want us to dig into her past

dig out *vtsep* (**a**) (*remove by digging*) dig out the roots; (**b**) (*release by digging*) they hope to have the remaining survivors dug out by nightfall; (**c**) (*find by searching hard*) have you dug those files out yet?; we want more information on the company's early days, so see what you can dig out

dig up *vtsep* (**a**) (*remove by digging*) this rose bush will have to be dug up and moved; (**b**) (*find*) we're hoping to dig up some items to show that there was a Roman encampment here; I've dug something up that might prove he's been lying to us

dip into *vipo* (**a**) (*place briefly*) she dipped her toes into the bath water to test it; (**b**) (*use part of*) she doesn't want to dip into her savings if she can help it; (**c**) (*read parts of*) this is the kind of anthology to be dipped into rather than read all at once

dish out *vtsep* (**a**) (*serve*) Mum's dishing supper out now; (**b**) (*give, especially in a negative sense*) you're very good at dishing out advice

dish up **1** *vtsep* (*place in dishes*) somebody dish up the soup; **2** *vi* (*serve food*) when will you be dishing up?

dispense with *vipo* (*do without*) he called it 'dispensing with my services' – I call it the sack

dispose of *vipo* (**a**) (*get rid of*) dispose of your waste paper here; **(b)** *Sl* (*kill*) we have to dispose of him before he talks; **(c)** (*beat*) so far she has disposed of six opponents who want to take the title away from her

divide out *vtsep* (*distribute*) they divided the food out

divide up *vtsep* (*separate*) contestants will be divided up into groups of four

do away with *vipo* **(a)** (*abolish*) they should do away with school; **(b)** (*kill*) he has threatened to do away with himself

do by *vipo Fam* (*treat*) the company did very badly by its employees; she did very well by her grand-daughter at Christmas; he'll feel very hard done by if you don't at least send him a birthday card

do down *vtsep* **(a)** (*cheat*) why did you let the salesman do you down?; **(b)** (*say bad things about*) there's always someone ready to do you down

do for *vipo Fam* **(a)** (*murder*) if he keeps on treating her this way, she'll do for him; **(b)** (*exhaust*) it was that last hill that did for me; **(c)** (*clean house for*) who does for you?

do in *vtsep Fam* **(a)** (*murder*) somebody on our street was done in last night; **(b)** (*exhaust*) Christmas shopping always does me in

do out *vtsep* (*clean, tidy*) will you do the kitchen out tomorrow please Mrs Jones?

do out of *vipo Fam* (*cheat*) he always maintained that he had been done out of his fair share of the inheritance

do over *vtsep* **(a)** (*redecorate*) the whole house needs doing over; **(b)** *Fam* (*beat up*) the other gang did him over; **(c)** *Am* (*repeat*) the teacher said I had to do my project over

do up 1 *vi* (*fasten*) clothes that do up at the front pose fewer problems for people in wheelchairs; **2** *vtsep* **(a)** (*fasten*) do your buttons up; **(b)** (*wrap*) it seems a pity to open it when it's done up so nicely; **(c)** (*improve appearance of*) they're doing up all the buildings on the street; you've really done yourself up – what's the occasion?

do with *vipo* **(a)** *used with 'could'* (*need*) you could do with a haircut; what I could be doing with right now is a hot bath; **(b)** (*be connected with*) he has something to do with computers; it sounds very fishy to me and you should have nothing to do with it; that's got nothing to do with it!; it has to do with your mother, I'm afraid; my business has nothing to do with you; **(c)** (*finish*) I've done with trying to help people; he says it's all over – he's done with her; **(d)** (*finish using*) if you've done with the hammer, put it back where it belongs

do without *vipo* (*manage without*) we can do without the sarcasm; if you don't find anything you like in here then you'll have to do without

double back **1** *vi* (*retrace footsteps*) they felt they ought to double back since they didn't recognize any landmarks; **2** *vtsep* (*fold back*) double back the bedclothes and let the mattress air

double over/up *vi* (*bend at waist*) the pain struck again and she doubled over; the joke made me double up

double up *vi* (*share bed, room etc*) with so many guests coming, some of them are going to have to double up; do you mind doubling up with me?

drag behind **1** *vtsep** (*pull, referring to something heavy*) I made for the bus stop, dragging my cases behind me; **2** *vi* (*lag*) you're dragging behind in maths

drag in *vtsep* **(a)** (*pull inside*) the trunk is too heavy to lift – let's just drag it in; **(b)** *Fam* (*refer to*) why do you have to drag in the one mistake I made?

drag on *vi* (*last a long time, too long*) the play dragged on and on

drag out *vtsep* (*cause to last long time*) I had to drag my presentation out to fill the time allotted to me

drag up *vtsep* **(a)** (**bring by pulling*) drag it up the stairs; **(b)** *Fam* (*take, cause to go*) you dragged me up to London for this?; **(c)** (*refer to*) there's no need to drag up the past; **(d)** *Fam* (*raise badly*) those children are being dragged up, not brought up; where were **you** dragged up?

draw alongside *vi* (*come up next to in vehicle*) then this big Mercedes drew alongside . . .

draw away **1** *vi* **(a)** (*move off*) the car drew away from the kerb; **(b)** (*move ahead*) the first half dozen runners are now beginning to draw away; **(c)** (*move away*) I can't help drawing away when he touches me; **2** *vtsep* (*lead away*) she drew us away from the other guests

draw back **1** *vi* (*recoil*) she drew back from the edge of the cliff; **2** *vtsep* **(a)** (*attract back*) what drew you back to music?; **(b)** (*open*) he draw back the curtains and light flooded into the room

draw in **1** *vi* **(a)** (*arrive*) the train will be drawing in soon; **(b)** (*become shorter*) the days have started to draw in again; **2** *vtsep* **(a)** (*pull inwards*) fresh air from outside is drawn in by these ventilators; **(b)** (*involve*) they were arguing again and I left because I didn't want to be drawn in

draw on **1** *vi* **(a)** (*approach*) as summer drew on . . .; **(b)** (*go past slowly*) as the day gradually drew on; **2** *vipo* (*use*) for this essay, I want you to draw on your own childhood memories; **3** *vtsep* (*put on*) she drew on a pair of long white gloves

draw out 1 *vi* **(a)** (*leave*) they waved as the train drew out; **(b)** (*become longer*) after Christmas, the days start to draw out; **2** *vtsep* **(a)** (*take out*) she drew out a gun; I've drawn out all my savings; **(b)** (*prolong*) they drew the meeting out on purpose; **(c)** (*cause to speak, implying that someone is reluctant*) I managed to draw her out on her plans

draw up 1 *vi* (*stop, in car*) he drew up with a squeal of brakes; **2** *vtsep* **(a)** (*formulate*) I think we should draw up a plan of action; the old lady drew up a new will; **(b)** (*bring up/over*) draw up a chair and join us

dream away *vtsep* (*spend time dreaming*) he'll dream his whole life away at this rate

dream up *vtsep* (*devise*) they've dreamed up some scheme that they say will make us all rich

dredge up *vtsep* **(a)** (*remove from river bed*) the barges are dredging up silt; **(b)** (*find, in a negative sense*) where did you dredge that old scandal up?

dress up 1 *vi* **(a)** (*wear elegant clothes*) for that special occasion when you want to dress up . . .; **(b)** (*wear fancy dress*) it's a Hallowe'en party and everybody has to dress up; **2** *vtsep* **(a)** (*wear elegant clothes*) she dressed herself up for the wedding; **(b)** (*in fancy dress*) you could dress yourself up as Pierrot

drink down *vtsep* (*swallow*) drink this down and you'll soon feel better

drink in *vtsep* (*absorb*) these plants will drink in as much water as you care to give them; *Fig* I'm drinking in your every word

drink up 1 *vi* (*finish drink*) drink up and I'll get the next round; **2** *vtsep* (*finish*) have you drunk up your tea?

drive at *vipo* (*mean, imply*) I'm sorry, but I really don't see what you're driving at; did you think she was driving at something when she said she couldn't afford a holiday this year?

drive back **1** *vi* (*return by vehicle*) are you driving back or taking the train?; **2** *vtsep* **(a)** (*return by vehicle*) George will drive you back to your hotel; **(b)** (*repel*) the soldiers did not have the strength to drive back another attack

drive home *vtsep* **(a)** (*force into place*) once you have driven the screws home . . .; **(b)** (*make understand*) I tried to drive it home to them that this was not an isolated incident

drive off **1** *vi* (*leave by vehicle*) he drove off about an hour ago; **2** *vtsep* **(a)** (*remove in vehicle*) all three of them were driven off in an unmarked police car; **(b)** (*repel*) the attackers were driven off when reinforcements arrived

drive on **1** *vi* (*continue to drive*) he decided to drive on rather than stop there for the night; **2** *vtsep* (*incite*) her friends drove her on to sue

drive up *vi* (*arrive*) a car has just driven up

drop back *vi* (*lose ground*) he has dropped back and it looks as if he's given up the race

drop behind **1** *vi* (*lag*) you're dropping behind – do try to keep up; **2** *vipo* that last lap took its toll and now she's dropping behind the leaders

drop in **1** *vi* (*visit casually*) I'll drop in and see mother tomorrow; would you drop in at the supermarket on your way home?; **2** *vtsep** (*deposit*) drop this in the night safe for me, will you?

drop off **1** *vi* **(a)** (*fall off*) with all this heavy shopping to carry, I feel as if my arms are going to drop off; **(b)** (*fall asleep*) it was 4 am before she dropped off; why don't you go to bed instead of dropping off in the chair?; **(c)** (*decline*) church attendance has been dropping off for many years;**2** *vtsep* (*deposit*) drop these books off at the library; (*let out of car etc*) where do you want to be dropped off?

drop out **1** *vi* **(a)** (*fall out*) there's a hole in your pocket and the keys must have dropped out; **(b)** *Fam* (*stop attending school etc*) he dropped out at the age of 14; so many have dropped out that the course may be cancelled; in the sixties a lot of people dropped out (*of society*) and went off to places like India

drum into *vtaspo* (*repeat until learned etc*) drum it into them that they mustn't take sweets from strangers

drum up *vtsep* (*generate, develop, find*) how are you drumming up support for the campaign?; we must drum up some more business

dry off **1** *vi* (*become dry*) don't touch the varnish while it's drying off; **2** *vtsep* (*make dry*) come and dry yourself off in front of the fire

dry out **1** *vi* **(a)** (*become dry*) leave your wet things in the bathroom to dry out; **(b)** (*lose alcohol from system*) I think she's somewhere drying out; **2** *vtsep* (*make dry*) soap can dry your skin out

dry up **1** *vi* **(a)** (*become dry*) streams and rivers are drying up because of this long heat wave; **(b)** (*stop speaking*) she was haunted by the thought that she might dry up in the middle of her big speech in the second act; **(c)** *Sl* (*be quiet*) why don't you dry up?; **2** *vtsep* (*make dry*) dry the bathroom floor up

dwell (up)on *vipo* (*think about, spend time on*) get on with your life instead of dwelling on what might have been

E

ease off/up *vi* (*slow down*) he's been told to ease off if he doesn't want a heart attack; ease up – there's a 30 mile an hour limit here

eat away *vtsep* (*erode*) the action of the waves is eating the coastline away

eat in *vi* (*eat at home*) I'm tired of eating in all the time

eat into *vipo* (*diminish*) long term unemployment eats into people's self-confidence; it's silly to eat into your savings when you could get a bank loan

eat out **1** *vi* (*eat in restaurant*) let's eat out tonight; **2** *vtsep* (*set phrase*) the child is eating her heart out (*ie longing*) for a pony

eat up **1** *vtsep* (*consume*) eat up your spinach; jealousy is eating him up; **2** *vi* (*finish eating*) eat up, there's lots more

edge out **1** *vi* (*leave cautiously*) I opened the window and cautiously edged out; **2** *vtsep* **(a)** (*leave cautiously*) she edged her way out on to the ledge; **(b)** (*supplant*) there's a move to edge him out of the chairmanship

egg on *vtsep* (*encourage*) it was sickening to hear the crowd egg the boxers on; I wish I hadn't let you egg me on to accept

end up *vi* (*finish*) no-one ever thought she would end up in prison; how did the film end up?; I ended up telling him in no uncertain terms what I thought

enter into *vipo* **(a)** (*begin*) we entered into this contract with our eyes open; now that you are about to enter into holy matrimony . . . (*ie get married*); **(b)** (*have a part in*) morality rarely enters into foreign policy

enter (up)on *vipo* (*commence*) she has entered on a new career

even out 1 *vi* (*become level*) production figures are evening out at about 5,000 per week; 2 *vtsep* (*make equal*) we have to even out the burden of caring for the handicapped

even up *vtsep* **(a)** (*make equal*) that last goal evened up the score; if you pay for the meal, that will even things up; **(b)** (*increase*) I hate these odd pennies – just even it up to a pound

explain away *vtsep* (*provide explanation for so as to make seem unimportant*) he tried to explain away his absence from the last meeting; explain this away if you can

eye up *vtsep Sl* (*look at*) I passed the time eyeing up all the men; he eyed up every single woman at the party

F

face up to *vipo* **(a)** (*accept*) we'll have to face up to the fact that we're not getting any younger; **(b)** (*confront*) it might help if she faced up to her fears of rejection

fade away *vi* (*disappear slowly*) the sound of the procession faded away; old soldiers never die, they merely fade away

fade in 1 *vi* (*appear slowly*) the music faded in; 2 *vtsep* (*cause to appear slowly, especially in a film*) fade in the crowd scenes

fade out 1 *vi* (*disappear slowly*) the music fades out for the last few seconds; 2 *vtsep* (*cause to disappear, especially in a film*) fade out the crowd scenes

fall about *vi* (*laugh heartily*) her scripts always make me fall about

fall away *vi* **(a)** (*go down steeply*) be careful – the ground falls away here; **(b)** (*decline*) attendance at committee meetings has been falling away recently

fall back *vi* (*retreat a little*) the demonstrators fell back when they saw the water cannon

fall back on *vipo* (*use in emergency*) I suppose we can always fall back on temporary staff

fall behind *vi* **(a)** (*not stay with the leader*) he began well but now seems to be falling behind (*ie in a race*); **(b)** (*not stay up to date*) you mustn't fall behind with the payments

fall down *vi* **(a)** (*fall to ground*) he fell down and bumped his head; **(b)** (*collapse*) why don't they demolish that old building instead of letting it fall down?; **(c)** (*fail*) that's where their argument falls down; if you fall down on this, she won't give you another chance

fall for *vipo* **(a)** (*be attracted to*) he has fallen for the girl next door; I've really fallen for that Victorian chair in the antique shop; **(b)** (*be deceived by*) you didn't fall for that old story, did you?

fall in with *vipo* **(a)** (*accept*) I fell in with the plans for a picnic because the children were so keen; **(b)** (*associate with*) the teenager next door has fallen in with a bad crowd

fall off *vi* **(a)** (*fall from something*) I was terrified of falling off and clung to the chimney for dear life; **(b)** (*decline*) enrolment is falling off

fall on *vipo* **(a)** (*be responsibility of*) if anything goes wrong you can be sure that the blame will not fall on him; **(b)** (*attack*) they fell on the meal as if they hadn't eaten for days

fall out *vi* **(a)** (*fall from*) the window is open so be careful you don't fall out; **(b)** (*quarrel*) my sister and I have fallen out

fall over 1 *vi* (*topple*) the vase is top-heavy, that's why it keeps falling over; **2** *vipo* **(a)** (*stumble on*) move your suitcase before someone falls over it; **(b)** (*be eager*) he was falling over himself to buy the woman a drink

fall through *vi* (*collapse*) their plans for a skiing holiday have fallen through

farm out *vtsep* (*ask others to deal with*) if deadlines are to be met then some of the work will have to be farmed out; those two next door are always farming their kids out

feed in *vtsep** (*enter, especially into a computer*) the keyboarders feed the data in

feed up *vtsep* (*fatten*) Mum always wants to feed us up when we come home for the weekend

feel up *vtsep Fam* (*touch without permission*) I slapped his face for feeling me up

feel up to *vipo* (*be able to cope with*) I don't feel up to cooking tonight – let's go out; he suggested a long walk but she didn't feel up to it; do you feel up to a visit from my mother?

fetch up 1 *vi* (*arrive*) we eventually fetched up in a tiny little village in the middle of nowhere; the road was very icy and they fetched up in a ditch; **2** *vtsep* (*vomit*) he fetched up his dinner

fiddle about/around *vi* **(a)** (*tinker*) he fiddled about for ages and still couldn't get the car to go; **(b)** (*waste time*) why don't you stop fiddling about and get down to some work?

fight back 1 *vi* **(a)** (*retaliate*) everybody encounters a bully at some time – you must learn to fight back; **(b)** (*rally*) he has been ill but is now fighting back; **2** *vtsep* (*suppress*) I fought back my anger and tried to answer calmly

fight down *vtsep* (*suppress*) you must fight down these fears

fight off *vtsep* (*repel*) government troops have fought off a number of attacks; his bodyguards had to fight off over-eager fans

fight on *vi* (*continue to fight*) she regards this as merely a setback and is determined to fight on

fight out *vtsep* (*settle by fight*) you'll have to fight this one out; I left them to fight it out

figure on *vipo* (*plan on*) I didn't figure on your mother coming too; he didn't figure on a woman for the position

figure out *vtsep* **(a)** (*understand*) she can't figure you out at all; **(b)** (*work out*) how did you figure it out that he was the culprit?; we figured out that they must be paying three times as much rent as we are

fill in **1** *vi* (*act as replacement*) this isn't her normal job – she's just filling in; who'll be filling in for you while you're on holiday?; **2** *vtsep* **(a)** (*make level*) workmen are filling those potholes in at last; **(b)** (*complete*) I must have filled in twenty forms; **(c)** (*inform*) will someone please fill us in on what's been happening?; **(d)** (*use up*) are you busy or just filling in time?

fill out **1** *vi* (*get plump*) he's beginning to fill out at last after his long illness; **2** *vtsep* (*complete*) will you fill out this form please?

fill up **1** *vi* (*become full*) the room was filling up; **2** *vtsep* **(a)** (*make full*) fill her up (*ie petrol in car*); let me fill your glass up; **(b)** (*complete*) there are one or two forms to be filled up first

filter out **1** *vi* (*leave slowly*) mourners filtered out of the church; information is beginning to filter out that . . .; **2** *vtsep* (*remove with a filter*) filter out the solids

find out 1 *vtsep* (*discover*) I could have found that out for myself; 2 *vi* (*discover*) has your wife found out yet?

finish off *vtsep* (**a**) (*complete*) let me just finish this chapter off; finish off your lunch; (**b**) (*have the last of*) you can finish off the cream if you like; (**c**) (*exhaust*) all that heavy digging has finished him off; (**d**) (*kill*) the men were finished off with a bullet through the skull; 2 *vi* (*end*) what did you have to finish off with?

finish up 1 *vtsep* (**a**) (*complete*) finish up your lunch; (**b**) (*have the last of*) don't finish up the pie; 2 *vi* (*end up*) we finished up in the pub down the road; he'll finish up in court; any more of this and I'll finish up a nervous wreck

fire away *vi Fam* (*begin, especially to talk or to ask questions*) fire away – I'm all ears

fish out *vtsep* (**a**) (*remove from water*) they fished him out of the river; (**b**) (*remove*) just let me fish the keys out

fish up *vtsep* (*bring up*) she fished her purse up from the bottom of the bag

fit in 1 *vtsep** (*find room/time for*) could you fit this pair of shoes in the case?; the hairdresser says she can fit me in tomorrow; 2 *vi* (**a**) (*go into place*) they won't fit in; (**b**) (*agree*) that doesn't fit in with what I was told; (**c**) (*harmonize*) how does that fit in with your plans?; I hate parties like this – I never feel that I fit in

fix on 1 *vtsep** (*attach*) he fixed the handle on for me; 2 *vipo* (*choose, decide*) have you fixed on a date yet?

fix up 1 *vtsep* (**a**) (*erect, fit*) the marquee will be fixed up on their front lawn; (**b**) (*arrange*) I've fixed up a blind date for you; (**c**) (*provide*) our in-laws will fix us up with a bed; **(d)** (*improve, especially referring to appearance*) they're busy fixing up the house; if you're going out, don't you think you should fix yourself up a bit first?; **2** *vi* (*arrange*) I'm sorry but I've already fixed up to go out

fizzle out *vi* (*die away*) people's enthusiasm is starting to fizzle out; all those big plans we had have just fizzled out

flag down *vtsep* (*stop*) it's impossible to flag a taxi down when it's raining

flake out *vi Fam* (*fall asleep, collapse*) six late nights in succession – no wonder you flaked out; I just want to flake out on the couch

flare up *vi* **(a)** (*burst into flames*) the fire flared up, turning night into day; **(b)** (*erupt*) the argument flared up when she said something about favouritism; he flares up at the least little thing (*ie becomes angry*)

flip over **1** *vtsep* (*turn over*) do you want your egg flipped over?; she was flipping over the pages of a magazine; **2** *vi* (*turn over*) the plane just seemed to flip over

float (a)round *vi* **(a)** (*circulate*) rumours have been floating around about your resignation; **(b)** (*drift*) I'm just floating around until my sister comes out of the hairdresser's

flood in *vi* (*arrive in great quantity*) when she opened the door, water flooded in; people are flooding in to see this film; light flooded in through the windows

flood out *vtsep* (*force to leave*) thousands of people in Bangladesh have been flooded out

fly in **1** *vi* (*arrive by air*) the royal visitors will fly in tomorrow; **2** *vtr* (*convey by air*) the army will fly troops in if necessary

fly off *vi* **(a)** (*leave by air*) they flew off in a helicopter; **(b)** (*be blown off*) his toupee flew off in the wind

fly out **1** *vi* (*depart by air*) the President flew out this morning; which airport are you flying out of?; **2** *vtsep* (*convey by air*) troops are being flown out as quickly as possible; the company is flying her out to be with her husband

fly past **1** *vipo* (*pass in a plane*) the squadron will fly past the airfield at precisely two o'clock; **2** *vi* (*elapse quickly*) the weekend has just flown past

fold away **1** *vi* (*fold up for storage*) does this table fold away?; **2** *vtsep* (*store*) fold your clothes away neatly; she folded the tablecloth away

follow on *vi* **(a)** (*come after*) you go ahead – we'll follow on; **(b)** (*continue*) how did the story follow on?; **(c)** (*result*) it follows on from this that . . .

follow out *vtsep* (*execute*) he followed out his plans

follow through **1** *vtsep* (*execute*) she firmly intends to follow the idea through; **2** *vi* (*complete swing*) the problem is that you're not following through after you hit the ball

follow up **1** *vtsep* **(a)** (*pursue*) the police are following up a number of leads; I want you to follow the matter up; **(b)** (*reinforce*) he followed up his complaint to the shop with an angry letter to the manufacturer; **2** *vi* (*reinforce, add to previous action*) he followed up with a right to the jaw

fool around *vi* **(a)** (*waste time*) parents are always worried about their kids fooling around; **(b)** (*act foolishly*) don't fool around with that glue or you'll get it all over you; **(c)** *Fam* (*have affair*) she thinks her husband is fooling around

fork out 1 *vtsep* (*provide, especially unwillingly*) I suppose Daddy forked out the cash for the repairs to your new Porsche; **2** *vi* (*pay money*) we're all going to have to fork out

freak out *vi Sl* (*become excited/cross*) Mum will freak out when she sees that you've dyed your hair blue

frighten away *vtsep* (*scare*) don't look so grim or you'll frighten people away

frown on *vipo* (*disapprove of*) they all frowned on my suggestion; her parents frowned on her marriage to a man so much younger

G

gain on *vipo* (*reduce distance between*) they're gaining on us

gear up **1** *vi* (*prepare*) the shops are already gearing up for Christmas; **2** *vtsep* (*prepare*) businesses are getting geared up for 1992

get about *vi* **(a)** (*be active, move around*) he doesn't get about much these days; **(b)** (*spread*) a rumour has got about that you're leaving

get across **1** *vi* **(a)** (*succeed in crossing*) there are no traffic lights there so I found it difficult to get across; **(b)** (*communicate with*) she can't get across to her audience; **2** *vtas* **(a)** (*convey*) because of flooding, they will be unable to get much needed supplies across the river; **(b)** (*communicate*) did you get it across to her just how important it was?

get along *vi* **(a)** (*leave*) I must be getting along. **(b)** (*be on good terms*) I wish I got along better with my neighbours; **(c)** (*cope, manage*) how are you getting along in the new house?

get around 1 *vi* **(a)** (*be active, be socially active*) handicapped people who find it hard to get around; that young man really gets around!; **(b)** (*spread*) I wonder how that story got around?; **2** *vipo* (*avoid, circumvent*) there's no getting around it, you'll have to tell him what happened; can we get around this difficulty?

get at *vipo* **(a)** (*find*) their house is very easy to get at; **(b)** (*discover*) he intends to get at the truth; **(c)** (*imply*) do you mind telling me what you're getting at?; **(d)** (*criticize*) his father is always getting at him for the length of his hair; **(e)** *Fam* (*influence, especially unfairly*) the trial could not continue because a number of witnesses had been got at and refused to testify

get away **1** *vi* **(a)** (*leave*) I usually get away by six; will they manage to get away this year?; **(b)** (*escape*) the terrorists got away in a stolen car; **2** *vtas* (*remove*) the policeman managed to get the gun away

get away with *vipo* **(a)** (*escape with*) the thieves got away with the old lady's life savings; **(b)** (*be let off with*) he got away with a small fine of £10; **(c)** (*not be punished for*) that child gets away with murder! (*ie can do anything without being punished*)

get back **1** *vi* **(a)** (*return*) when did you get back?; I must be getting back soon; **(b)** (*move away*) get back from the edge of the cliff!; **2** *vtsep* **(a)** (*succeed in removing*) the priest got the distraught woman back from the window ledge by promising that something would be done; **(b)** (*recover*) I'll get it back from him tomorrow; **(c)** (*return*) get the file back to me as soon as you can

get back at *vipo* (*have revenge*) I'll get back at you for that

get back to *vipo* **(a)** (*return*) I must get back to work soon; **(b)** (*contact*) can we get back to you on that point later?

get behind 1 *vi* (*become delayed*) I've got so behind that I'm working late every night this week; **2** *vipo* (*move to the back of*) get behind that tree

get by 1 *vi* **(a)** (*succeed in passing*) the car could not get by because of the roadworks; **(b)** (*manage*) he thinks he'll get by without studying; it must be difficult getting by on so little money; do you think I'll get by in Greece without speaking the language?; **2** *vipo* **(a)** (*move past*) can I get by you?; **(b)** (*escape attention of*) his latest book did not get by the censor

get down 1 *vi* **(a)** (*descend, from wall, tree etc*) get down at once!; **(b)** (*duck*) get down or she'll see us; **(c)** (*leave the table*) may I get down?; **2** *vtsep* **(a)** (*lower*) will you get my case down for me?; **(b)** (*reduce*) the doctors have got his temperature down at last; **(c)** (*make a note of*) I'll get that down if you'll give me a moment; **3** *vtas* **(a)** (*depress*) this kind of weather gets everybody down; **(b)** (*swallow*) her throat is so swollen she can't get anything down; get this soup down and you'll soon feel better;

get down to *vipo* (*tackle*) when are you going to get down to your homework?

get in 1 *vtsep* **(a)** (*summon*) I was so worried about the baby that I got the doctor in; **(b)** (**bring inside*) just let me get the washing in before the rain starts; farmers are only now getting their crops in; **(c)** (*plant in the ground*) you should get your bulbs in earlier than this; **(d)** (*manage to do*) she got some last-minute revision in the night before the exam; **(e)** (*insert*) she was talking so much I couldn't get a word in; **2** *vtas* **(a)** (*ensure admission to*) these excellent exam results will get you in anywhere (*referring to university*); **(b)** (*ensure election of*) it was the government's mistakes that got the opposition in; **3** *vipo* (*enter*) get in the car!; the smoke from the camp fire got in their eyes; **4** *vi* **(a)** (*arrive*) when does the train get in?; he got in before I did; **(b)** (*gain entrance*) if they didn't have a key, how did they get in?; **(c)** (*be elected*) she got in with a very small majority

get in on *vipo* (*take part in*) they'd all like to get in on the deal

get into **1** *vipo* **(a)** (*put on*) she hasn't been able to get into any of her clothes since the baby was born; **(b)** (*affect*) I don't know what's got into her these days; **(c)** (*set phrases*) there's no need to get into a panic; you'll get into trouble for that; they've got badly into debt; **(d)** (*learn*) she'll soon get into our ways; **(e)** (*become interested in*) everyone says this is an excellent book, but I just can't get into it; **(f)** (*gain entrance*) only a small percentage of candidates get into university; the thieves got into the house through an open window; **2** *vtaspo* **(a)** (*involve*) you got me into this mess, now get me out; **(b)** (*cause to be*) she knows just what to do to get her father into a good mood; don't get her into one of her rages

get in with *vipo* **(a)** (*be on good terms with*) if you want to get in with him, tell him how much you enjoyed his singing; **(b)** (*associate with*) she's worried about her daughter getting in with a bad crowd

get off **1** *vi* **(a)** (*descend from vehicle*) he got off at the traffic lights; **(b)** (*leave, especially referring to work*) I'd like to get off early tomorrow; **(c)** (*escape unpunished*) he shouldn't have got off; you got off lightly!; **(d)** (*fall asleep*) I couldn't get off at all last night; **2** *vtas* **(a)** (*send*) it's time to get the children off to bed; I must get this letter off in time to catch the last post; **(b)** (*remove*) you should have got that off your desk by now; get your hands off that child; get those football boots off the chair; **(c)** (*save from punishment*) he has a reputation for always getting his clients off (*said of a lawyer*); **(d)** (*have as holiday*) maybe I could get the afternoon off; **(e)** (*obtain*) I got it off the woman next door; **(f)** (*free from*) the burns were not very serious but they got him off work; **(g)** (*put to sleep*) it always takes ages to get her off

get off with *vipo* **(a)** (*establish relationship with, in sexual sense*) trust her to get off with the only decent looking chap here; **(b)** (*escape serious punishment*) he got off with just a fine

get on **1** *vi* **(a)** (*enter bus/train*) where did you get on?; **(b)** (*progress*) if he wants to get on, the best thing he can do is work hard; **(c)** (*age*) my grandmother is getting on; **(d)** (*become late*) time is getting on; **(e)** (*have good relations*) we don't get on; **(f)** (*cope*) how did you get on at the dentist's? (*ie how did it go?*); how is the old man going to get on without his dog?; **2** *vtsep** (*put on*) I can't get the lid on; once you get your coat on, will you start the car?; you won't be able to get that on the bus, it's far too big; I got her on (the train) with seconds to spare

get on for *vipo* (*approach*) she must be getting on for 90 but she's very active; it's getting on for four o'clock; there were getting on for 500 guests at the wedding

get on to *vipo* **(a)** (*locate, find name of*) how did you get on to me?; **(b)** (*contact*) I'll get on to the bank about it; **(c)** (*move forward*) I'd like to get on to the question of expenses

get on with *vipo* **(a)** (*continue with*) please get on with what you are supposed to be doing; I would like to get on with my reading; that will do to be going on with; **(b)** (*progress*) how are you getting on with the painting?; **(c)** (*have good relationship with*) I don't get on with my parents

get out 1 *vi* **(a)** (*leave*) I told her to get out; **(b)** (*be released*) when does he get out?; **(c)** (*be socially active*) she doesn't get out much; he ought to get out more; **(d)** (*leak*) how did the news get out?; **2** *vtsep* **(a)** (*extract*) I got my purse out to pay the milkman; get your books out and turn to page 54; **(b)** (*free*) our prime concern must be to get the hostages out; **(c)** (*produce*) he couldn't get a word out when they told him his wife had had triplets; we have to get this report out by Monday; **(d)** (*eliminate from cricket match*) John got their best batsman out for ten

get out of 1 *vipo* **(a)** (*extricate oneself from*) he always gets out of the washing up; **(b)** (*become unaccustomed to*) I've got out of the habit of studying; she has got out of the way of doing dishes without a dishwasher; **(c)** (*leave*) let's get out of here; he got out of the country before the police came looking for him; the children get out of school at about three o'clock; **2** *vtaspo* **(a)** (*derive*) I don't see what pleasure he gets out of all this studying; she really gets the most out of life, doesn't she?; **(b)** (*extract*) get the big pot out of the cupboard; the detective finally got the truth out of the suspect

get over 1 *vi* **(a)** (*cross*) you get over first; **(b)** (*communicate*) she cannot get over to her audience; **2** *vipo* **(a)** (*recover from*) he hasn't got over the shock of his wife's death yet; I'm getting over it gradually; **(b)** (*conquer*) she gave an excellent speech once she got over her difficulties with the microphone; you must get over these silly fears; **3** *vtas* (*transport*) it's not easy getting fifty children over a busy road; **4** *vtsep* (*convey, communicate*) you got your point over very well

get over with *vtas* (*complete, referring to something unpleasant*) once I got my appointment with the dentist over with, I thoroughly enjoyed my day off; can we get this over with quickly?

get round **1** *vi* **(a)** (*arrive*) the vet said she'll get round as soon as she can; **(b)** (*spread*) the news is getting round; **2** *vipo* **(a)** (*circumvent*) there's no getting round it – you'll have to own up; how did they get round the export regulations?; **(b)** (*cajole*) I can always get round my father; **3** *vtas* (*persuade*) you've got me round to your way of thinking

get round to *vipo* (*do, often referring to something difficult or boring*) I'll get round to it eventually, I promise

get through **1** *vi* **(a)** (*make telephone call*) the lines must be down, I can't get through; **(b)** (*arrive*) will the message get through?; the cars could not get through because the pass was blocked with snow; **(c)** *Am* (*finish*) the evening class does not usually get through until nine o'clock; **(d)** (*pass exam*) only three of the class didn't get through; **2** *vipo* **(a)** (*negotiate successfully*) you will not be able to get through the roadblock; **(b)** (*succeed in*) I got through my exams second time around; **(c)** (*finish*) will you get through your home work in time to come to the match?; **(d)** (*use up*) he gets through a dozen shirts a week; since she retired, she's been finding it difficult to get through the days; **4** *vtas* **(a)** (*cause to succeed*) it was your essay that got you through (the exam); **(b)** (*transport successfully*) they got the food supplies through just in time; **(c)** (*make comprehensible*) I finally got it through to him that I wasn't interested

get to *vipo* **(a)** (*reach*) how do we get to their house from here?; **(b)** (*begin*) you know, I've got to wondering if maybe he isn't right after all; **(c)**

(*upset, make an impression on*) she really got to me with her sarcastic remarks; you shouldn't let it get to you; **(d)** (*manage to, be able to*) did you actually get to speak to the Prime Minister?

get together 1 *vi* (*meet*) when can we get together to discuss the project?; he's getting together with the bank manager tomorrow; **2** *vtsep* (*collect*) get your things together

get up 1 *vi* **(a)** (*rise*) it's time to get up (*ie from bed*); he got up to address the audience (*ie stood up*); **(b)** (*develop*) there's a storm getting up; **2** *vtsep* **(a)** (*generate*) we'll get up speed when we reach the motorway; **(b)** (*organize*) we've got up a petition to protest about the closure; **3** *vtas* **(a)** (*rouse*) will you get me up early tomorrow?; **(b)** (*move up*) help me get this up; **(c)** (*dress up*) she's getting herself up as Cleopatra

get up to 1 *vipo* **(a)** (*reach*) it took ages to get up to the top; **(b)** (*create*) those children are always getting up to mischief; I don't want you getting up to anything while I'm out; **2** *vtas* (*carry up*) get this up to the top bedroom for me

give away *vtsep* **(a)** (*donate*) I gave it away to someone who needed it more; **(b)** (*distribute*) a former pupil is giving the prizes away; **(c)** (*give in marriage at a wedding ceremony*) her uncle is to give her away; **(d)** (*betray*) who gave us away?; she gave the game away by telling him about the party

give in 1 *vtsep* (*hand over*) give your homework in; I gave the wallet in to the police; **2** *vi* (*surrender*) I give in – tell me what the answer is; Oscar Wilde said that the only way to get rid of temptation was to give in to it

give off *vtr insep* (*emit*) this fire gives off a lot of heat; something is giving off a bad smell

give on to *vipo* (*face*) the windows give on to the main road so it's a noisy flat

give out 1 *vtsep* **(a)** (*distribute*) they were giving out leaflets about abortion; **(b)** (*make known*) the Chancellor gave out the trade figures today; **(c)** (*emit*) the radiators are not giving out much heat; **2** *vi* **(a)** (*become used up*) supplies have given out; my patience is giving out; **(b)** (*break down*) the iron has given out

give over 1 *vtsep* **(a)** (*devote*) they gave the entire evening over to a discussion of the film; **(b)** (*transfer*) the vicar gave the hall over to the scouts; **2** *vi Fam* (*stop*) give over, will you!

give up 1 *vtsep* **(a)** (*abandon*) the climbers gave up hope of being found before nightfall; give it up as a bad job; **(b)** (*stop*) she is giving up chocolate as part of her diet; I've given up trying; **(c)** (*stop expecting*) we had almost given you up; **(d)** (*regard*) to give someone up as dead/lost; **(e)** (*surrender*) I gave up my seat on the bus to a pregnant woman; the escaped prisoner gave himself up after two days; **(f)** (*devote*) I gave the entire week up to studying; **2** *vi* (*surrender*) don't shoot – we give up; ok, tell me the answer then, I give up

give up on *vipo* (*stop hoping for*) how can a mother give up on her daughter and say she's no good?

give way *vi* **(a)** (*yield*) his mother gave way to grief when she heard what had happened; give way to oncoming traffic; **(b)** (*be superseded by*) my laughter gave way to tears; natural fibres have given way to synthetics

gloss over *vtsep* **(a)** (*make light of*) she very kindly glossed over my mistakes; I tend to gloss those things over; **(b)** (*try to hide*) he glosses over his past

go about 1 *vi* **(a)** (*move*) policeman always go about in pairs; you can't go about saying things about people like that; **(b)** (*date*) my son has been going about with her for a year now; **(c)** (*circulate*) there's a story going about that they've separated; there seems to be a virus going about; **2** *vipo* **(a)** (*tackle*) what's the best way to go about buying a house?; **(b)** (*conduct*) just go about your business as usual

go after *vipo* (*pursue*) go after them!; we are going after the big prize; she really goes after what she wants

go ahead *vi* **(a)** (*proceed*) if you have something to say to me, just go ahead!; they have decided to go ahead with the wedding; the project is going ahead quite satisfactorily; **(b)** (*go in front*) you go ahead, we'll follow later

go along *vi* **(a)** (*walk along*) she met him as she was going along the road; **(b)** (*proceed*) please check your punctuation as you go along; **(c)** (*agree*) I cannot go along with you on that; the specialist proposed therapy instead of surgery and his colleagues went along

go at *vipo* (*attack*) he went at the wall with a hammer; the children went at the cakes with a will

go back *vi* **(a)** (*return*) let's go back some day; **(b)** (*be returned*) when do these library books go back?; the sheets you bought will have to go back because there is a flaw in them; **(c)** (*be put back*) don't forget that the clocks go back tomorrow; **(d)** (*date back*) the church has records going back to the 16th century

go back on *vipo* (*abandon, alter*) I cannot go back on my promise to her; he never goes back on his decisions

go by **1** *vi* **(a)** (*pass*) as the parade was going by . . .; **(b)** (*elapse*) many years have gone by since we met!;

(c) (*allow to escape*) don't let this opportunity go by; 2 *vipo* (a) (*judge on the basis of*) don't go by my opinion – I hate that kind of film; if you go by that clock, you'll miss the train; (b) (*follow*) he never goes by the rules; go by your brother's example; (c) (*be known as*) she has been going by her maiden name since the divorce

go down *vi* (a) (*set*) the sun is going down; (b) (*sink*) the ship went down with all hands; (c) (*decline*) house prices may go down; flood waters are going down; (d) (*be defeated*) I won't go down without a fight; (e) (*be pleasing*) my suggestion did not go down very well; British television programmes always go down big in North America; how did your suggestion go down?; (f) (*be swallowed*) this wine goes down very nicely, don't you think?; some water will help the pill go down; (g) (*lose status*) my old neighbourhood has really gone down; his family has gone down in the world since losing all their money; she went down in my estimation when I found out what really happened; (h) (*be remembered*) how will Ronald Reagan go down in history?; (i) (*fall ill*) trust me to go down with flu on the day of the exams

go for *vipo* (a) (*attack*) what was I supposed to do when she went for me with a knife?; go for him, boy!; billiard players always go for the balls in a certain order; (b) (*strive to attain*) if you really want it, go for it!; with his next jump, he's going for the gold; (c) (*be attracted to*) I could go for you in a big way; she's always gone for the Scandinavian type

go in for *vipo* (a) (*enter for*) are you going in for the three hundred metres?; (b) (*participate in, use, take pleasure in*) he doesn't go in for team sports; why do scientists go in for all that jargon?; my parents don't go in for pop music; (c) (*pursue as* *career/hobby*) they have decided to go in for catering

go into *vipo* **(a)** (*enter*) our special training programme is now going into its third year; she has to go into hospital; he nearly went into hysterics at the thought of it; **(b)** (*have as career*) she wants her daughter to go into teaching; **(c)** (*examine*) we won't go into that for the moment; **(d)** (*embark on*) my grandmother then went into a long and detailed description of her childhood; **(e)** (*wear*) their son did not go into long trousers until he was fifteen

go off **1** *vi* **(a)** (*depart*) she has gone off with the man next door; he's gone off on some business of his own; **(b)** (*deteriorate, go bad*) the milk has gone off; your work has gone off recently – is anything wrong?; **(c)** (*sound*) the alarm went off at the usual time; he said that the gun just went off in his hand; **(d)** (*cease working*) the lights went off all over the city last night; **(e)** (*be received*) how did the play go off?; my presentation went off well/badly; **2** *vipo* (*lose liking for*) I've gone off him since I found out what a male chauvinist pig he is; she says she has gone off Spain

go on **1** *vi* **(a)** (*continue*) go on – what did he say then?; just go on with what you were doing; do we have enough coffee to be going on with or should I buy some more?; **(b)** (*fit*) your coat won't go on unless you wear a different sweater; **(c)** (*begin to operate*) the street lights go on when it gets dark; **(d)** *Fam* (*talk non-stop*) once he starts, he goes on and on; my aunt keeps going on at me about getting a job; **(e)** (*happen*) what's going on?; **(f)** (*pass*) as time went on, I realized that . . .; **2** *vipo* **(a)** (*begin*) most people go on a diet at least once; he goes on unemployment benefit next week; **(b)** *Fam* (*like*) my sister is really gone on the boy next door; **(c)** (*be guided by*) I have nothing concrete to go on – I just don't trust him; **(d)** (*approach*) she's two years old, going on three

go out *vi* **(a)** (*leave*) they were just about to go out; **(b)** (*leave house*) she has decided to go out to work; we're going out for dinner; **(c)** (*date*) she first went out with him six months ago; **(d)** (*be defeated*) I bet his team goes out in the first round; **(e)** (*be extinguished*) put some wood on the fire before it goes out; the lights went out; **(f)** (*be sent, especially from an organization*) has that letter gone out?; **(g)** (*set phrase*) (*go to sleep*) I went out like a light; **(h)** (*become unfashionable*) the stores are betting on the miniskirt not going out for another year; **(i)** (*ebb*) the tide has gone out

go over **1** *vi* **(a)** (*cross*) I went over and tapped him on the shoulder; **(b)** (*transfer*) they've gone over to the Conservative Party; he's thinking about going over to cigars; **(c)** (*be received*) my suggestion didn't go over at all well; **2** *vipo* **(a)** (*examine*) we should go over the accounts; **(b)** (*rehearse*) let's go over your speech a second time; **(c)** (*discuss*) we must have gone over this point a dozen times already

go round **1** *vi* **(a)** (*spin*) everything is going round; **(b)** (*make detour*) the policeman said we would have to go round; **(c)** (*visit*) you ought to go round and see him; she's gone round to her mother's; **(d)** (*suffice*) there won't be enough to go round; **2** *vipo* **(a)** (*detour*) I went round the long way to be sure of not getting lost; **(b)** (*tour*) we must have gone round every museum in town; she went round the neighbourhood looking for her cat; **(c)** (*be sufficient for*) is the roast big enough to go round everyone?

go through 1 *vi* (*be completed*) the deal has gone through; when does the divorce go through?; **2** *vipo* **(a)** (*suffer*) she has gone through a lot; **(b)** (*examine*) the detective went through the witness's statement very carefully; **(c)** (*search*) I've gone through all the papers and I still can't find it; **(d)** (*rehearse*) how often do you have to go through your lines before you know them by heart?; **(e)** (*use up*) children go through a lot of shoes; we've gone through six pints of milk in two days

go through with *vipo* (*carry out*) he decided at the last moment that he couldn't go through with the wedding; management went through with its threat to close the factory

go together *vi* **(a)** (*harmonize*) do these colours go together?; **(b)** (*go out with boyfriend/girlfriend*) we've been going together for a long time

go towards *vipo* (*contribute*) the proceeds from the fete are going towards a new village hall

go under **1** *vi* **(a)** (*sink in water*) it's too late – he's gone under; **(b)** (*fail*) his business is going under and there isn't much he can do about it; **2** *vipo* (*be known as*) since the divorce she's been going under her old name of Williams

go up *vi* **(a)** (*go upstairs, climb*) just go up – he's expecting you; **(b)** (*increase*) the patient's temperature had been going up and up; house prices are going up again; **(c)** (*rise*) the curtain will go up at eight o'clock (*ie in theatre*); **(d)** (*be destroyed*) the building went up in flames; *Fig* his plans went up in smoke

go with *vipo* **(a)** (*accompany*) mathematical skills usually go with an ability to play chess; **(b)** (*harmonize with*) change your tie – it doesn't go with that shirt; **(c)** (*be included in price of*) do the carpets go with the house?

go without 1 *vi* (*not have*) those are too dear – if you don't like any of the others you'll just have to go without; 2 *vipo* (*not have*) I went without breakfast so I wouldn't be late

grow apart *vi* (*become distant*) they have grown apart over the years

grow in (*grow back*) your hair will grow in soon

grow out of *vipo* **(a)** (*become too large for*) he has grown out of those shoes we bought just a few months ago; **(b)** (*become too old for*) I've grown out of my friends; when are you going to grow out of biting your nails?

grow up *vi* **(a)** (*become adult*) children grow up so fast nowadays; **(b)** (*behave like adult*) I wish you would grow up!; **(c)** (*develop*) a theory has grown up that . . .

guard against *vipo* (*be careful to avoid*) take vitamin C to guard against colds

H

hammer home *vtsep* **(a)** (*insert fully with hammer*) be sure to hammer all the nails home; **(b)** (*insist on*) we hammered home the importance of wearing seat belts

hammer out *vtsep* **(a)** (*remove with hammer*) I'll have to hammer these dents out; **(b)** (*draw up, implying difficulty*) they have finally managed to hammer out an agreement on the withdrawal of troops

hand back *vtsep* (*return*) I'll hand it back to you as soon as I've finished

hand down *vtsep* **(a)** (*take from high place*) hand that plate down to me; **(b)** (*bequeath*) she handed the necklace down to her granddaughter; **(c)** (*pronounce*) the sentence will be handed down soon

hand in *vtsep* (*deliver*) I want you to hand in your essays tomorrow

hand out *vtsep* **(a)** (*distribute*) I've offered to hand leaflets out; **(b)** (*give*) you can always rely on him to hand out advice

hand over **1** *vtsep* **(a)** (*deliver*) she handed the papers over to the lawyer for safekeeping; **(b)** (*give up*) hand over your wallet; **(c)** (*transfer*) we now hand you over to our foreign affairs correspondent; he will be handing over the reins of power very soon; **2** *vi* **(a)** (*give up*) I know you have it, so hand over!; **(b)** (*transfer*) I now hand over to the weatherman; when will he be handing over to the new chairman?

hang about/around **1** *vi Fam* **(a)** (*wait*) I had to hang about for ages before he finally arrived; now hang about, that isn't what she said!; **(b)** (*dawdle*) don't hang about or we'll never finish; **2** *vipo* (*frequent, with negative implications*) I don't want you hanging about amusement arcades

hang back *vi* (*be reluctant*) there's always one child who hangs back when Santa Claus is handing out the presents; if you have a contribution to make to the discussion, please don't hang back; I hung back from saying anything because . . .

hang down *vi* (*descend*) her hair hung down in ringlets

hang in *vi Sl* (*not lose heart, persevere*) hang in there, boys – we'll get you out soon; he'll just have to hang in until a better job comes along

hang on **1** *vi* **(a)** (*hold*) hang on tight; **(b)** (*wait*) can you hang on for a couple of minutes?; **2** *vipo* **(a)** (*be attentive to*) the audience was hanging on the speaker's every word; **(b)** (*depend on*) the fate of the project hangs on the availability of supplies

hang on to *vipo* **(a)** (*cling to*) he hung on to the cliff face; **(b)** (*keep*) I'd hang on to those documents if I were you

hang out *vi* **(a)** (*be visible*) your shirt tails are hanging out; **(b)** *Fam* (*frequent*) I'm looking for Bill – any idea where he hangs out?; **(c)** *Fam* (*be stubborn in order to obtain*) I'm hanging out for a rise

hang together *vi* (*be consistent*) the plot of the film doesn't hang together

hang up **1** *vi* (*replace telephone receiver*) don't hang up until you've heard what she has to say; hang up immediately; **2** *vtsep* (*place on peg*) hang your coat up

happen along *vi* (*arrive by chance*) then, thank goodness, a policeman happened along

hark back *vi* (*recall*) he keeps harking back to the Blitz

have around *vtas* **(a)** (*keep available*) it's always a good idea to have some candles around; **(b)** (*invite*) we must have them around for supper soon

have back **1** *vtsep* (*retrieve*) I'll have my book back please; **2** *vtas* (*invite in return*) we're having them back next Saturday

have in *vtas* **(a)** (*summon*) we'll have to have the plumber in to fix that leak; **(b)** (*invite*) the old ladies across the street like having people in for tea; **(c)** (*set phrase*) (*have a grudge against*) to have it in for someone; I really think he has it in for me the way he keeps criticizing my work

have off *vtas* **(a)** (*remove*) the doctor had the plaster off in no time at all; **(b)** (*have removed*) she's having the plaster off next week; **(c)** *Sl* (*have sex*) those two look as if they have it off every night

have on **1** *vtsep* **(a)** (*wear*) he looks totally different when he has something casual on; **2** *vtas* **(a)** *Fam* (*tease*) didn't you realize I was having you on?; **(b)** (*have arranged*) she has a lot on this week; I have something else on, I'm afraid; **(c)** (*have information about*) he told the police they had nothing on him – he'd been in hospital at the time; **(d)** (*install*) once we have the roofrack on, we'll be all set

have out *vtas* **(a)** (*have extracted*) he's in hospital having his appendix out; **(b)** (*settle argument*) let's have this out once and for all

have up *vtas* **(a)** (*bring to court*) the two old tramps were had up for vagrancy; **(b)** (*erect, install*) they worked all night to have the exhibits up in time for the opening

head for *vipo* **(a)** (*go to*) where is he headed for?; let's head for home; **(b)** (*approach*) she's heading for a disappointment if she thinks he's going to propose; the country is heading for civil war

head off *vtsep* **(a)** (*divert*) head Mum off for a couple of minutes while I finish wrapping her present; **(b)** (*forestall*) to head off accusations of favouritism . . .

head up *vtsep* (*act as head of*) how many committees does she head up?

hear of *vipo* (*allow*) I won't hear of you going to a hotel

hear out *vtsep* (*listen to end of speech*) please hear me out; the committee heard her out before reaching a decision

heat up **1** *vi* **(a)** (*become warm*) you will soon heat up; **(b)** (*become animated*) the discussion heated up and turned into an argument; **2** *vtsep* (*warm*) heat up some milk; a bowl of soup will heat you up

hide out *vi* (*be in hiding*) he's hiding out in some hotel to get away from his fans

hit back 1 *vi* (*reply*) he has questioned my integrity and I firmly intend to hit back; 2 *vtsep* (*return by hitting*) hit the ball back

hit off *vtsep* (a) (*imitate, in drawing, impersonating etc*) he hits the prime minister off very well; (b) (*set phrase*) (*have good relationship*) we hit it off immediately; she and her father don't hit it off

hit out *vi* (*attack*) all of the speakers at the conference hit out at the proposals

hit on *vipo* (*discover*) I've hit on a possible solution

hive off 1 *vi* (*diversify*) they're hiving off into the retail side of things; 2 *vtsep* (*separate*) my boss is furious that the company wants to hive off the research team

hold against *vtaspo* (*criticize for*) why do you hold my past against me?; I hold it against him that . . .

hold back 1 *vi* (a) (*stay in background*) I held back while the two of them discussed old times; (b) (*restrain oneself*) he held back for a time but finally spoke his mind; 2 *vtsep* (a) (*restrain*) marshals held the fans back; he held back his rage; (b) (*impede*) it's your poor performance in maths that is holding you back; (c) (*withhold*) she's holding something back, I know she is; don't hold anything back

hold down *vtsep* (a) (*restrain*) the government must take action to hold down interest rates; it took two of us to hold him down; (b) (*have or keep, referring to jobs*) she is holding down a fairly high-powered job in the City; (*keep*) can he hold this job down?

hold forth *vi* (*speak pompously*) she held forth at great length on the benefits of fresh air

hold in *vtsep* (*restrain*) for heaven's sake, hold your stomach in; she shouldn't hold her emotions in

hold off 1 *vi* (*keep away*) the rain seems to be holding off; 2 *vtsep* (*keep back*) the remaining men managed to hold off the attack until reinforcements arrived

hold out 1 *vi* **(a)** (*last*) our supplies will not hold out for long; **(b)** (*endure*) can you hold out until the doctor gets here?; 2 *vtsep* **(a)** (*stretch out*) she held out her hand; **(b)** (*offer*) the doctor doesn't hold out much hope for a complete recovery

hold out on *vipo* (*keep information from*) you've been holding out on me – I didn't know you played the saxophone

hold to *vipo* (*abide by*) he held to his decision

hold up 1 *vi* **(a)** (*stay up*) the centuries-old house continues to hold up; **(b)** (*stay calm*) she held up magnificently under the strain; 2 *vtsep* **(a)** (*raise*) she held her face up to the sun; **(b)** (*support*) what's holding the tent up?; **(c)** (*delay*) bad weather is holding the project up; **(d)** (*rob*) armed men held up another bank yesterday

hold with *vipo* (*approve of*) I don't hold with all these fancy names for children

hole up *vi Fam* (*hide*) he decided to hole up for a while

home in on *vipo* (*reach or find accurately*) the missiles can home in on the heat of aircraft engines; she homed in on my one mistake

hook up 1 *vi* **(a)** (*fasten by means of hook*) the dress hooks up; **(b)** (*connect*) we will be hooking up with European networks to bring you this very special programme; 2 *vtsep* (*fasten, referring to dress etc*) hook me up

hot up *Fam* 1 *vi* (*intensify*) the argument hotted up when . . .; things are hotting up again on the labour relations front; 2 *vtsep* (*intensify*) they are hotting up the pace

hunt down *vtsep* **(a)** (*search for*) they are being hunted down by state and federal police; **(b)** (*find*) he was finally hunted down

hunt out *vtsep* (*find*) I've hunted out those old family photographs you wanted to see

hurry along **1** *vi* (*move quickly*) hurry along please, the museum is now closed; you're hurrying along as if we were late; **2** *vtsep* (*cause to move more quickly*) I'm trying to hurry the project along but it's not easy; you can't hurry these things along

hurry up **1** *vi* (*move more quickly*) do hurry up or we'll be late; **2** *vtsep* (*cause to move more quickly*) I'll go and hurry them up; could you hurry things up a bit please – this is my lunch hour

I

ice over *vi* (*be frozen*) this river is too fast flowing to ever ice over

ice up *vi* (*become covered with ice*) the crash was attributed in part to the plane's wings having iced up; I can't get the key in – the lock must have iced up

improve on *vipo* (*make better*) I told him you can't improve on perfection; she'll have to improve on that score with her next jump

iron out *vtsep* **(a)** (*remove with iron*) I'll iron out these creases in your shirt for you; **(b)** (*resolve*) there are one or two little problems that must be ironed out; have you ironed out your differences?

J

jack in *vtsep Sl* **(a)** (*give up*) I'm going to jack this job in as soon as I can; **(b)** (*stop*) jack it in!

jack up	*vtsep* **(a)** (*raise by means of jack*) he had to jack up the car to change the wheel; **(b)** *Fam* (*increase*) they've jacked up the price of petrol again
jam in(to)	**1** *vtsep** (*squeeze in*) can you jam anything else in?; **2** *vi* (*squeeze in*) hundreds of people jammed in to hear her speech
jam on	*vtsep* (*put on with force*) I had to jam on my brakes or I would have hit him; *she jammed her hat on and marched out
jam up	*vtsep* (*block*) Sunday motorists in search of a good spot for a picnic have jammed up the roads
jar on	*vipo* (*irritate*) that constant banging is jarring on my nerves
jazz up	*vtsep Fam* (*enliven*) it's very dull in here tonight – couldn't we jazz things up a bit?; jazz up a plain dress with some costume jewellery
jockey for	*vipo* (*manoeuvre to obtain*) everyone is jockeying for the position of chairperson
jockey into	*vtaspo* (*manoeuvre into*) they jockeyed me into volunteering my services
jog along	*vi* (*move at steady pace*) the work is jogging along
join in	**1** *vi* (*take part*) I want everyone to join in; **2** *vipo* (*take part in*) I joined in the fun; they all joined in the chorus
join on	**1** *vi* (*attach*) where does this bit join on?; **2** *vtsep** (*attach*) they've joined on another carriage
join up	**1** *vi* **(a)** (*enlist in the army etc*) he joined up as soon as war was declared; **(b)** (*meet*) the two detachments will join up here; **2** *vtsep* (*connect*) join the ends up
jot down	*vtsep* (*write quickly*) he jotted down a few notes

for his speech; just jot it down

jump at *vipo* (*accept eagerly*) I jumped at the chance of a holiday in Spain; when he offered her the position, she jumped at it

jump down **1** *vi* (*descend by jumping*) there aren't any steps – you'll have to jump down; he jumped down from the window; **2** *vipo* (*set phrase*) (*criticize*) she's always jumping down my throat about something

jump on **1** *vi* (*enter by jumping*) there was a bus sitting at the traffic lights so he decided to jump on; **2** *vipo Fam* **(a)** (*attack*) the hooligans jumped on the old man at the corner of the street; **(b)** (*criticize*) he jumps on me for the least little thing

K

keel over *vi* **(a)** (*overturn*) the lifeboat keeled over; **(b)** (*faint*) he keels over at the sight of blood

keep at **1** *vipo* **(a)** (*continue to work at*) if he wants to get into university, he'll have to keep at his maths; **(b)** (*nag*) the pair of them kept at me, morning noon and night; **2** *vtaspo* (*compel to work*) the pile-up on the motorway kept the operating staff at it all night; he's kept us hard at it all morning

keep away **1** *vi* (*stay at a distance*) I knew you had visitors so I kept away; she can't keep away from chocolates; **2** *vtas* (*keep at a distance*) keep him away from me; it must be a really important case if it's keeping her away this long

keep back **1** *vi* (*stay away*) a policeman was telling people to keep back; **2** *vtsep* **(a)** (*restrain*) the marshals at the rock concert had a job keeping the fans back from the stage; **(b)** (*withhold*) I couldn't keep back my tears; she's keeping something back from us; **(c)** (*not allow to move to a higher* *class*) we do not like keeping children back but in this case feel we have no alternative; **(d)** (*delay*) am I keeping you back?

keep down **1** *vi* (*stay low*) keep down or he'll see us; **2** *vtas* **(a)** (*lower*) the policemen surrounding the house were told to keep their heads down; please keep your voice down – some people are trying to concentrate; **(b)** (*retain food*) the doctor was worried that her patient couldn't keep anything down; **3** *vtsep* **(a)** (*repress*) it's a full-time job keeping the weeds down in this garden; **(b)** (*contain*) the government is not doing anything to keep inflation down; he's trying hard to keep his weight down but he's not having much success

keep from **1** *vtaspo* **(a)** (*conceal*) they kept the news from the old lady as long as possible; what are you keeping from me?; **(b)** (*prevent*) the climber hung on to his partner's hand to keep him from going over the edge; **(c)** (*distract from*) I mustn't keep you from your work; **(d)** (*protect*) I'm trying to keep you from harm; **2** *vipo* (*refrain*) he was such a boring speaker that I couldn't keep from nodding off

keep in with *vipo* (*stay on good terms with*) if you want to keep in with him, just agree with everything he says

keep off **1** *vi* (*stay away*) that's my tree house – keep off! **2** *vipo* (*stay away from*) keep off the grass; they tactfully kept off the subject of divorce; the doctor has ordered him to keep off the port and cigars; **3** *vtaspo* (*not touch*) Mum said to keep our hands off the cakes; **4** *vtas* (*remove, not wear*) don't keep your coat off for long or you'll get cold

keep on **1** *vi* **(a)** (*continue*) if they keep on like this much longer, I'm going to call the police; are you sure you told her she had to keep on past the war memorial?; **(b)** (*nag*) the headmaster keeps on at his pupils about their behaviour at the bus stop; it doesn't do any good to keep on about his drinking; **2** *vtsep* **(a)** (*retain in employment*) do you want to keep the cleaning woman on?; **(b)** (**continue to wear*) make sure the baby keeps her gloves on

keep out **1** *vi* **(a)** (*stay away*) danger – keep out!; the poacher kept out of sight until the gamekeeper had finished his round; **(b)** (*not become involved*) I'm keeping out of this argument; **2** *vtsep* **(a)** (*put at a distance*) lock the door to keep people out; keep plastic bags out of the reach of children; these boots are supposed to keep the rain out; **(b)** (*not involve*) I'll do my best to keep you out of this

keep to **1** *vipo* **(a)** (*honour*) people should keep to their promises; **(b)** (*not leave*) she's keeping to the house on doctor's orders; keep to the right; we must keep to the agenda and not go off at tangents all the time; **2** *vtaspo* **(a)** (*hold*) be sure to keep her to her promise; we are endeavouring to keep delays to a minimum; **(b)** (*not reveal*) please keep the news to yourself; he can't keep anything to himself

keep up **1** *vi* **(a)** (*continue*) if this snow keeps up much longer the roads will be blocked; **(b)** (*remain level, go at same speed*) she dictated so quickly that her secretary couldn't keep up; **(c)** (*remain in contact*) do you keep up with them?; **2** *vtsep* **(a)** (*continue*) we kept up a fairly regular exchange of letters until quite recently; it seems impossible for him to keep this pace up; keep it up, you're doing fine; **(b)** (*maintain in good condition*) her arthritis prevents her keeping up the garden the way she would like; **(c)** (*stop from falling*) keep your spirits up; he has lost so much weight he finds it difficult to keep his trousers up; **(d)** (*stop from going to bed*) our dinner guests kept us up until three o'clock this morning

kick about/around **1** *vi* **(a)** *Fam* (*lie unused*) don't leave the paper kicking about; **(b)** (*not be busy*) find yourself something to do instead of kicking around; **2** *vtsep* **(a)** (**move by kicking*) they're not doing any harm kicking a ball around; **(b)** (*bully*) you've kicked me around long enough; **(c)** *Fam* (*discuss*) we kicked the proposal around for a while but finally decided against it

kick in *vtsep* (*destroy by kicking*) the soldiers kicked the door in; I'll kick his teeth in!

kick off **1** *vi* **(a)** (*begin football game*) when do they kick off?; **(b)** *Fam* (*begin*) our speaker will now answer questions – who's going to kick off?; let's kick off with a situation report; **2** *vtsep** **(a)** (*remove by kicking*) it's always such a relief to kick your shoes off; **(b)** (*expel*) they're going to kick him off the team for misconduct

kick out **1** *vi* (*strike out with foot*) the mules kicked out whenever anyone approached; **2** *vtsep Fam* (*expel*) his wife has kicked him out and he's got nowhere to go

kick up *vtsep* (*create, referring to trouble etc*) he'll kick up an awful fuss when he finds out

knock about/around **1** *vi* = **kick about/around 1**; **2** *vtas Fam* **(a)** (*beat*) he knocks her about regularly; **(b)** (*damage*) the car was knocked about a good bit but the driver is unharmed

knock back *vtsep* **(a)** (*drink quickly*) he's knocking them back a bit, isn't he?; **(b)** *Fam* (*cost*) how much did that knock them back?

knock down *vtsep* **(a)** (*demolish*) the council wants to knock those houses down; **(b)** (*cause to fall*) the car that knocked her down was moving much too fast; the champion knocked his opponent down in the first round; **(c)** (*persuade to reduce price*) we're trying to knock them down to something we can afford; **(d)** (*reduce price of*) she knocked it down a fair bit; **(e)** (*sell at auction*) both paintings were knocked down to dealers

knock off 1 *vi Fam* (*stop work*) I'll try to knock off early; **2** *vtsep* **(a)** (**cause to fall*) the cat must have knocked it off; **(b)** (**lower price by*) could you knock a pound or two off?; **(c)** (*do quickly*) she knocks those sketches off by the dozen; **(d)** *Sl* (*steal*) those watches that he's trying to sell have probably been knocked off; **(e)** *Sl* (*murder*) she's terrified he'll be knocked off for informing; **(f)** *Sl* (*stop*) knock it off you two!

knock out *vtsep* **(a)** (*empty by knocking*) knocking his pipe out, he said . . .; **(b)** (*make unconscious*) will they knock you out or just give you a local anaesthetic?; the challenger knocked the champion out with a single punch; **(c)** (*eliminate*) that's her knocked out of Wimbledon already!; **(d)** *Fam* (*exhaust*) those children have knocked me out; **(e)** (*cause to fail*) the storm has knocked out power supplies to a great many homes; **(f)** *Fam* (*fill with delight*) his performance can hardly be described as knocking the critics out

knock over *vtsep* (*cause to fall*) he knocked several people over as he ran away; a bus knocked her over; *it wasn't me that knocked the ornament over

knock together **1** *vi* (*strike together*) my knees were knocking together at the thought of the interview; **2** *vtsep* (*make hurriedly*) I've promised to knock a tree house together for the kids

knock up **1** *vi* (*prepare for ball game*) the players are allowed two minutes to knock up; **2** *vtsep* **(a)** *Br* (*waken*) will you knock me up at six o'clock?; **(b)** *Am Fam* (*make pregnant*) he's knocked her up; **(c)** (*make hurriedly*) if you don't mind leftovers,

I'll knock a quick meal up for you

know of *vipo* **(a)** (*be aware of*) has Bill arrived? – not that I know of; **(b)** (*have heard of*) nothing is known of her whereabouts; I don't know him, I know of him

knuckle under *vi* (*submit*) I won't knuckle under to threats

L

lash down **1** *vtsep* (*tie down*) the lorry driver lashed the tarpaulin down; **2** *vi* (*rain heavily*) it's lashing down

lash into *vipo* **(a)** (*attack physically*) the two men lashed into each other; **(b)** (*attack verbally*) I lashed into her for making such silly mistakes

lash out **1** *vi* **(a)** (*attack*) he lashed out at me with a chain; she lashes out at anyone who opposes her; **(b)** *Fam* (*spend, implying a lot of money*) I think I'll lash out and treat myself to a new coat; **2** *vipo* (*spend, implying large sums of money*) they lashed out a couple of thousand on that holiday to the States

last out **1** *vi* **(a)** (*survive*) they can't last out for long in this weather unless they find shelter; **(b)** (*be sufficient*) will our water last out?; **2** *vtsep* **(a)** (*survive*) she is not expected to last out the night; **(b)** (*be sufficient*) we have coal to last out the winter

laugh off *vipo* (*dismiss as being ridiculous*) he laughed off all warnings

launch into *vipo* (*begin with eagerness*) he launched into a glowing description of the car he had just bought

launch out *vi* **(a)** (*diversify*) the company is going to launch out and add textiles to its product range; **(b)** (*make new beginning*) this brilliant young chef intends to launch out on his own some day

lay about *vipo* (*attack*) the old lady laid about him with her stick

lay down *vtsep* **(a)** (*put down*) he laid his glass down on the table; **(b)** (*give up*) the rebels have announced that they will lay down their arms; she laid down her life for her beliefs; **(c)** (*fix, especially by law or rules*) it is laid down in the regulations; don't lay the law down to me

lay in *vtsep* (*obtain and store*) we have laid in enough canned goods to feed an army; you had better lay some wood in

lay off **1** *vi Fam* (*stop*) I've had as much criticism as I can take, so lay off; **2** *vipo Fam* (*stop bothering*) my sister doesn't want to go out with you so lay off her; **3** *vtsep* (*make redundant*) the company will be laying 350 employees off within the next few weeks

lay on *vtsep* (*supply*) water and electricity are both laid on at the cottage; extra buses will be laid on if necessary; I'll lay on a meal for everyone

lay out *vtsep* **(a)** (*spread out*) lay the pattern out on the floor; **(b)** (*prepare*) she always lays her clothes out the night before; **(c)** (*prepare for burial*) they laid Grandad out very nicely; **(d)** (*plan*) I don't like the way the office has been laid out; **(e)** (*knock unconscious*) he laid me out with one blow; **(f)** (*spend*) your parents have laid out a considerable sum on your education

lay up *vtsep* **(a)** (*confine to bed*) this flu has laid her up; **(b)** (*immobilize*) the severely damaged vessel will be laid up for repair

lead on **1** *vi* (*lead forward*) lead on!; **2** *vtsep* **(a)** (*deceive*) he led her on with promises of marriage; you led me on to believe that . . .; **(b)** (*influence*) it was those so-called friends of his that led him on to do it

lead up *vi* **(a)** (*precede*) in the years leading up to the Declaration of Independence . . .; **(b)** (*prepare for*) her opening remarks were plainly leading up to a full-scale attack on her critics; what's this leading up to?

lean on *vipo* **(a)** (*depend on*) his mother leans on him for advice; **(b)** (*pressurize*) the company is leaning on her to take early retirement

leave behind *vtsep* **(a)** (*not take*) drivers are advised to leave their cars behind and use public transport; **(b)** (*forget*) I came out in such a rush that I left my keys behind; **(c)** (*outstrip*) when it comes to maths, she leaves most of the others far behind

leave off **1** *vtsep** (*not put on*) it was such a beautiful day I left my coat off; who keeps leaving the lid off the coffee jar?; she wants to leave most of her relations off the guest list; **2** *vipo* (*stop*) he has left off seeing her; **3** *vi Fam* (*stop doing, especially something annoying*) leave off, will you!

leave out *vtsep* **(a)** (*omit*) you've left out an entire line; the old lady decided to leave her son-in-law out of her will; **(b)** (*not involve*) leave me out of this; **(c)** (*leave ready*) I'll leave out the instructions for the washing machine; **(d)** (*not put away*) do you want to leave the car out?

let down *vtsep* **(a)** (*lower*) they let a rope down to the men stranded on the beach; **(b)** (*disappoint*) you must stop letting people down like this; **(c)** (*lengthen*) she always lets down the hem on her daughter's dresses; **(d)** (*deflate*) the boys let his tyres down as a joke

let in **1** *vtsep* **(a)** (**allow to enter*) these shoes are letting water in; don't let him in; **(b)** (*tell*) they let me in on the secret; **2** *vi* (*admit water etc*) are your boots letting in?

let in for *vtaspo* (*cause*) your absence let us all in for a lot of extra work; he didn't realize what he was letting himself in for

let off *vtsep* **(a)** (*detonate*) animal rights activists have let off a number of bombs; **(b)** (*emit*) the fire was letting off a lot of smoke; **(c)** (*pardon, not punish severely*) he was let off because of lack of evidence; the judge let him off with a fine; **(d)** (*allow to leave*) the teacher lets us off early on Fridays; **(e)** (**deposit from vehicle*) I asked the taxi driver to let me off at the corner

let on *vi* **(a)** (*tell secret*) I'm pregnant but don't you let on; **(b)** (*pretend*) he likes to let on that he went to university

let out *vtsep* **(a)** (*allow to go out*) they're letting him out on parole soon; don't bother seeing me to the door, I'll let myself out; **(b)** (*reveal*) who let it out about the party?; **(c)** (*emit*) she let out a yelp of pain; **(d)** (*rent*) they let out rooms to students; **(e)** (*make larger*) I'm either going to have to go on a diet or let all my clothes out

let up *vi* (*cease*) I wish this rain would let up; don't you ever let up? (*ie stop doing something*)

lie back *vi* **(a)** (*recline*) you lie back and rest; **(b)** (*not act*) he just lay back and let the rest of us do the work

lie in *vi* (*stay in bed*) most people lie in on Sundays; I wish I could have lain in this morning

lie up *vi* **(a)** (*rest in bed*) the doctor says she's to lie up for a couple of days; **(b)** (*hide*) the police are convinced that the wanted men are lying up somewhere; **(c)** (*be unused*) that boat has been lying up for years

light up **1** *vi* **(a)** (*become bright*) his face suddenly lit up; the room seemed to light up when she came in; **(b)** (*start smoking*) he lit up and sighed with contentment; **2** *vtsep* **(a)** (*illuminate*) the fireworks lit up the sky; **(b)** (*start smoking*) they both lit up their pipes

line up 1 *vi* (*queue*) people are already beginning to line up outside the cinema; **2** *vtsep* **(a)** (*arrange in line*) the headmaster lined everybody up in the playground; **(b)** (*arrange*) I've lined a date up for you; he's got something else lined up for tomorrow

listen in *vi* (*listen to*) it's fascinating listening in on other people's conversations

live down *vtsep* (*be forgotten by other people*) we'll never live this scandal down; he won't let her live it down that she made one stupid mistake

live in/out (*live inside/outside place of work or study*) they have at least three maids living in; I would rather live out than stay in a hall of residence

live off *vipo* **(a)** (*use as food or money*) that child would live off ice cream if he could; she lived off what she earned as a cleaner; **(b)** (*use as source of money*) his brother lives off him

live on *vi* (*continue for a long time*) the memory of their sacrifice will live on

live up to *vipo* **(a)** (*meet*) nothing ever lives up to expectation; **(b)** (*emulate*) there's no point in trying to live up to my sister's reputation

load down *vtsep* (*be burdened*) I'm loaded down with shopping

load up 1 *vi* (*take on load*) there are a number of ships waiting to load up; **2** *vtsep* (*fill*) we loaded the car up with everything bar the kitchen sink

lock away *vtsep* (*make safe by locking*) lock those papers away for the night; the police said they could lock him away for ten years

lock in *vtsep** (*imprison*) she is locked in a cell with three other women; (*in room etc*) you almost locked me in

lock out *vtsep* (*exclude by locking*) they've gone to bed and locked me out; the company has threatened to lock its employees out unless they return to work immediately

lock up **1** *vi* (*make house secure*) you go to bed – I'll lock up; **2** *vtsep* (*secure by locking*) lock up your valuables; the dogs are locked up every night

long for *vipo* (*desire*) I'm longing for the holidays

look after *vipo* (*take care of*) we've been looking after our grandchildren for the weekend; the car has been well looked after

look at *vipo* **(a)** (*take a look*) look at those punks!; **(b)** (*inspect*) I'll need to get someone in to look at that damp patch; **(c)** (*consider, have attitude towards*) he doesn't look at it that way at all; **(d)** (*consider favourably*) he sent her the most beautiful flowers for her birthday but she still won't look at him

look back *vi* (*recall*) looking back, do you have any regrets?

look down on *vipo* (*scorn*) he looks down on anyone who hasn't gone to university

look for *vipo* (*seek*) I'm really looking for something a bit bigger

look forward to *vipo* (*anticipate with pleasure*) you must be looking forward to their visit

look in *vi* (*visit briefly*) I'll look in again tomorrow; they looked in for a minute

look into *vipo* (*investigate*) the company has promised that it will look into my complaint

look on **1** *vi* (*watch*) a crowd looked on as firemen fought the blaze; **2** *vipo* (*consider*) they look on her as a daughter; I used to look on him with envy

look on to *vipo* (*face*) our house looks on to open fields

look out **1** *vi* **(a)** (*look in outwards direction*) she opened the window and looked out; **(b)** (*be careful*) look out – you're very close to the edge; **2** *vtsep* (*search for and find*) look out a scarf for me; she has promised to look those letters out

look out for *vipo* **(a)** (*keep watch for*) you could always ask the garage to look out for a second-hand car; **(b)** *Am* (*take care of*) he promised his parents he would always look out for his younger brother

look over *vtsep* (*examine*) we're looking over a flat this evening; I'm sure I've been invited for the weekend just so his mother can look me over

look to *vipo* (*rely on*) you must stop looking to other people to solve your problems

look up **1** *vi* **(a)** (*raise head*) she looked up when I entered the room; looking up from his book, . . .; **(b)** (*improve*) his business must be looking up if he's bought a new car; **2** *vtsep* **(a)** (*visit*) you must look us up again; **(b)** (*seek*) look it up in the encyclopaedia

look up to *vipo* **(a)** (*look in upwards direction*) he's so tall I have to look up to him; **(b)** (*admire*) everyone looks up to her for her courage

loosen up **1** *vtsep* (*relax*) some massage will loosen you up; they've promised to loosen up the rules; **2** *vi* (*relax*) they'll take a couple of minutes loosening up (*ie warming up muscles, sportsmen etc*)

lose out *vi* (*come off worst*) you're the one who'll lose out; he lost out on a deal

louse up *vtsep Sl* (*spoil, do badly*) you're always lousing things up for me; he really loused that race up

M

make for *vipo* **(a)** (*head towards*) where are you making for?; **(b)** (*be likely to cause*) handling a complaint in that way does not make for good customer relations

make of *vipo* **(a)** (*understand by*) well, what do you make of that?; **(b)** (*consider as important*) you're making too much of this – I've known him since we were children; a lot has been made of this by the Press

make off *vi* (*escape*) the boys made off at a run when they saw the policeman

make off with *vipo* (*take, steal*) who's made off with the scissors again?; don't leave your bag lying around – someone might make off with it

make out **1** *vtsep* **(a)** (*write out*) make the cheque out to me; **(b)** (*discern*) can you make out who it is?; **(c)** (*decipher*) he can't make out his own handwriting; **(d)** (*understand*) I can't make her out at all; **2** *vi* (*fare*) how is she making out in her new job?; **3** *vipo* (*imply*) the insurance company is making out that I was negligent

make over *vtsep* (*transfer*) she has made her entire estate over to her granddaughter

make up **1** *vtsep* **(a)** (*apply make up to*) I must go and make my face up; **(b)** (*settle quarrel*) thank goodness they've made it up; **(c)** (*compensate for*) he doesn't have to worry about making up any losses since he comes from a wealthy family; overtime will be necessary to make up the ground we lost because of the weather; I promise I'll make it up to you; **(d)** (*invent*) she is making the whole thing up, it's not true; **(e)** (*form*) would you make these up into three separate packages?; the community is made up primarily of old people; **(f)** (*increase*) for your birthday, I'll make your savings up to the price of a new bike; **2** *vi* **(a)** (*settle quarrel*) haven't you two made up yet?; **(b)** (*catch up*) he's making up on the leaders

make up for *vipo* (*compensate for*) how can I make up for forgetting your birthday?; he's certainly making up for lost time now

make up to *vipo* (*flatter*) don't try making up to me; they got the money by making up to the old man

map out *vtsep* **(a)** (*make map of*) have you mapped out the route yet?; **(b)** (*plan*) I've mapped out a programme

mark up *vtsep* (*increase price of*) most restaurants mark up wine by about ten per cent

marry off *vtsep* (*dispose of by marriage*) she's being married off to a man who's twenty years older than her

measure up **1** *vtsep* **(a)** (*take measurements*) after measuring up the timber, . . .; **(b)** (*assess*) she measured the situation up with one glance; **2** *vi* (*be good enough*) I don't think you're going to measure up to the job

meet up *vi* (*meet*) let's meet up again soon

meet with *vipo* **(a)** (*encounter*) the proposal has met with fierce opposition; rescue attempts have so far met with failure; **(b)** (*have meeting with*) the senator is meeting with his advisors next week

melt away *vi* **(a)** (*disappear by melting*) the ice has melted away; **(b)** (*disappear*) the onlookers melted away after the initial excitement

melt down *vtsep* (*change shape by melting*) the gold jewellery will have been melted down by now and will be impossible to identify

mess about/around *Fam* **1** *vtsep* **(a)** (*treat badly*) first we're going, then we're not going – I wish you would stop messing me about!; **(b)** (*interfere with, change order of*) they've messed the programmes around again; **2** *vi* **(a)** (*play the fool*) stop messing about!; **(b)** (*do nothing constructive*) he's been messing about in the garden all day; **(c)** (*tinker*) don't mess around with something that doesn't belong to you

mess up *vtsep* **(a)** (*make untidy*) don't mess the kitchen up; **(b)** (*ruin*) you've really messed your marriage up; he's messed things up for all of us

miss out **1** *vtsep* (*omit*) have I missed anyone out?; **2** *vi* (*miss, implying something good has been missed*) you missed out on a great concert; you missed out there

mix up *vtsep* **(a)** (*prepare by mixing*) will you mix up some of my medicine for me?; **(b)** (*confuse*) don't talk to me when I'm trying to count or you'll mix me up; he mixes her up with her mother; **(c)** (*involve*) everyone in that family is mixed up in something dishonest

move along **1** *vtsep** (*cause to move*) policemen had to move the crowd along; **2** *vi* **(a)** (*move to make room*) move along and let the lady sit down; **(b)** (*leave*) I really ought to be moving along; all the policeman said of course was "move along, there's nothing to see"; **(c)** (*continue*) moving along to my next question . . .

move in **1** *vtsep* **(a)** (*send*) the government has decided to move troops in to quell the riots in the city; **(b)** (*take to new home*) the company can't move us in for another two weeks; **2** *vi* **(a)** (*advance, especially in a threatening way*) troops are now moving in on the beleaguered capital; **(b)** (*take up residence*) people are moving in next door

move on 1 *vtsep* (*cause to move*) the police moved us on; **2** *vi* (*advance*) can we move on to the next item on the agenda?

move out 1 *vtsep* (*remove*) you'll have to move the car out of the garage; they're being moved out of their homes to make way for a new road; the new government has promised to move its soldiers out; **2** *vi* **(a)** (*leave home*) the people next door have decided to move out; **(b)** (*withdraw*) troops are already moving out

move up 1 *vtsep* **(a)** (*change position of*) move this section up; his regiment was moved up to the front; **(b)** (*promote*) they've moved him up to be assistant manager; **2** *vi* (*advance*) troops are moving up to the combat zone

muddle along/on *vi* (*cope in haphazard fashion*) they were muddling along quite happily and then management brought in a team of consultants to look at efficiency

muddle up *vtsep* (*confuse*) he's managed to muddle the dates up; you're muddling me up

muscle in *vi Fam* (*force one's way in*) he's not keen on people muscling in on his territory; I'm not going to let anyone muscle in (*eg take over part of my job, benefits etc*)

N

narrow down 1 *vi* (*be reduced*) the question narrows down to this; **2** *vtsep* (*reduce*) we've narrowed the candidates down to four

nod off *vi Fam* (*fall asleep*) grandpa was sitting nodding off in front of the television

notch up *vtsep Fam* (*achieve*) she has notched up yet another win

O

open on to *vipo* (*face*) the back door opens on to a paved courtyard

open out **1** *vi* (*open completely*) the roses are beginning to open out; **2** *vtsep* (*unfold*) it's difficult to open out your newspaper on a crowded commuter train

open up **1** *vi* **(a)** (*open completely*) another couple of warm days and the roses will have opened up; **(b)** (*be frank about oneself*) he never opens up to anybody; **(c)** (*develop*) new markets are opening up all the time; **(d)** (*open closed door of house, shop*) police – open up!; she was just opening up when I passed; **(e)** (*start business*) there are some new shops opening up on the high street; **2** *vtsep* **(a)** (*make accessible*) the rain forest is being opened up for development; **(b)** (*open for business*) when did you open the shop up this morning?; **(c)** (*start business*) opening up a restaurant in this part of town is a risky venture

opt out *vi* (*choose not to participate*) I'm opting out of the committee because I have too many other commitments

own up *vi* (*confess*) I know it was you I saw so you might as well own up; he rarely owns up to his mistakes

P

pack away *vtsep* **(a)** (*store*) maybe we packed our winter clothes away a little too soon; **(b)** *Fam* (*eat a lot*) I've never seen anyone who can pack it away like you

pack in **1** *vtsep* **(a)** (**crowd in*) you can't possibly pack anything more in; **(b)** (*attract crowd*) her latest film is packing them in; **(c)** *Fam* (*stop*) he's decided to pack his job in; go next door and tell them to pack that noise in; **(d)** *Fam* (*stop seeing, referring to boyfriend/girlfriend*) are you going to pack him in or not?; **2** *vi* **(a)** (*crowd in*) I don't know how all those people manage to pack in on one train; **(b)** *Fam* (*stop working*) the lawnmower's packed in on me

pack off *vtsep* (*send, dispatch*) I'll call you back once I've packed the kids off to school

pack out *vtsep* (*fill completely*) the fans packed the hall out; the pub was packed out so we went somewhere else

pack up *vi* **(a)** (*prepare suitcases*) pack up – we're not staying here another night; **(b)** (*prepare to leave work*) are you packing up already?; **(c)** *Fam* (*stop working*) the lawnmower has just packed up so I can't cut the grass

palm off *vtsep Fam* **(a)** (*dispose of something unwanted*) they're palming the children off on us for the weekend; be careful he doesn't try to palm any rotten fruit off on you; **(b)** (*give something worthless to*) the last time I complained, the company palmed me off with a form letter

pass away *vi Euphemistic* (*die*) the old lady passed away in her sleep

pass by **1** *vi* **(a)** (*go past*) luckily a taxi was passing by just at that moment; **(b)** (*elapse*) time is passing by – are you going to meet the deadline?; **2** *vipo* (*go past*) we pass by that house every morning; **3** *vtas* (*ignore*) do you ever feel that life has passed you by?

pass off **1** *vi* **(a)** (*take place*) the ceremony passed off without a hitch; **(b)** (*end*) is the nausea passing off?; **2** *vtsep* (*pretend to be*) he passed her off as a duchess

pass on **1** *vi* **(a)** *Euphemistic* (*die*) when did your father pass on?; **(b)** (*proceed*) why don't we pass on to the next item on the agenda and come back to this later?; **2** *vtsep* (*tell or give to other people*) don't pass this on, but . . .; I passed the file on to him yesterday

pass out **1** *vi* (*faint*) one look at the needle and she passed out; I must have passed out; **2** *vtsep* (*distribute*) he passed copies of the memo out to the people at the meeting

pass over **1** *vtsep* (*ignore*) they've passed me over for promotion again; **2** *vi Euphemistic* (*die*) the clairvoyant began to talk about "our loved ones who have passed over"

pass up *vtsep* (*not take, implying foolishness or regret*) imagine passing up a job like that!; she has had to pass up the offer

patch up *vtsep* **(a)** (*repair temporarily*) I've managed to patch the car up so that it gets us into town at least; the army doctor just patched him up and sent him back to the front; **(b)** (*settle quarrel*) we had the most awful fight but we've patched things up now

pay back *vtsep* **(a)** (*return something that is owed*) have you paid that money back yet?; **(b)** (*have revenge on*) I'll pay you back for this!

pay off *vtsep* **(a)** (*dismiss with payment*) the company is going to pay half its labour force off at the end of the month; **(b)** (*finish paying*) when we've paid the mortgage off, . . . ; **(c)** (*bribe with money*) the policeman admitted to having been paid off

pay out *vtsep* **(a)** (*spend money, often unwillingly*) he's had to pay out a lot on car repairs lately; **(b)** (*count out money*) the wages were paid out this morning; **(c)** (*release gradually, usually referring to rope*) pay out some more line

pay up **1** *vtsep* **(a)** (*pay debt*) has she paid up what she owes you?; **(b)** (*pay for*) my subscription is paid up; **2** *vi* (*pay, often implying unwillingness or lateness on the part of the payer*) I've asked him twice to pay up but I'm still waiting

pick off *vtsep* **(a)** (**remove*) why spend all that time putting nail varnish on when you just pick it off a day later?; pick those papers off the floor; **(b)** (**pluck*) the birds have picked all the cherries off; **(c)** (*kill, especially with gun*) the sniper picked them off one by one

pick on *vipo* **(a)** (*select*) who have you picked on for your bridesmaid?; why pick on me to answer?; **(b)** *Fam* (*criticize, implying unfairness*) stop picking on the boy, he's doing his best

pick out *vtsep* **(a)** (*select from group*) I've picked out one or two patterns you might like; she picked the man out from an identity parade; **(b)** (*recognize*) I picked you out immediately – you were the only one wearing a red coat; **(c)** (*remove*) pick out any badly bruised fruit; **(d)** (*emphasize*) the panels on the door are picked out in a deeper shade of the colour used on the walls; **(e)** (*play in unskilled fashion on a musical instrument*) he can pick out a few tunes but that's all

pick up **1** *vtsep* **(a)** (*lift*) he picked up a book and started to read; **(b)** (*collect, often by vehicle when referring to people*) will you pick my prescription up at the chemist's?; when did he say he would be picking us up?; the bus stopped to pick up passengers; **(c)** (*acquire, often cheaply*) they picked that wonderful old table up at an auction; **(d)** *Fam* (*make a casual acquaintance of, especially with a view to sexual relations*) he goes around picking up women; **(e)** (*catch an illness or disease*) she's constantly picking up colds; **(f)** (*learn*) that child has picked up some very bad habits; I'll never pick this game up; **(g)** (*arrest*) he's been picked up for shoplifting; **(h)** (*continue with*) to pick up my story, . . .; **(i)** (*locate*) the police have picked up a trail that might lead them to the wanted man; you can pick up a lot of foreign stations with a short-wave radio; **(j)** (*correct*) please pick me up if I make any mistakes; **2** *vtas* (*make better, more cheerful*) a tonic will pick her up; what would really pick me up would be . . .; **3** *vi* **(a)** (*improve*) the weather is picking up; he's been quite ill but he's picked up in the last day or two; **(b)** (*continue*) let's pick up where we left off; **(c)** (*become acquainted with*) I don't like that crowd you've picked up with

pile up **1** *vi* (*accumulate*) the work tends to pile up at this time of year; one of the lanes has had to be closed and traffic is piling up; **2** *vtsep* (*accumulate*) pile the leaves up there; *Fam* they're piling up the money

pin down *vtsep* **(a)** (*trap*) they were pinned down by wreckage; he has his opponent pinned down on the canvas; **(b)** (*force someone to decide*) I've tried to pin her down about a time; **(c)** (*be definite about, identify*) it's just one of those feelings that are very difficult to pin down; I was sure I had seen him before but I couldn't pin him down

pipe down *vi Fam* **(a)** (*make less noise*) I wish you two would pipe down while I'm trying to watch television; **(b)** (*not talk*) just pipe down about it, OK?; he finally piped down when he realized she knew more about it than he did

play about/around *vi* (*not be serious*) it's about time he stopped playing about and settled down; you shouldn't play about with people's feelings

play along **1** *vi* (*co-operate*) if that's what you've decided then I'm quite happy to play along; **2** *vtas* (*manipulate, especially to gain advantage*) he's just playing her along until he gets what he wants

play back *vtsep* (*play again, of recording*) play that last bit back

play down *vtsep* (*minimize importance of*) she played down the extent of her injuries; the government is trying to play down its involvement

play off **1** *vtsep* (*oppose, especially in order to gain a personal advantage*) she's playing Phil off against Tom; you take pleasure in playing people off against each other, don't you?; **2** *vi* (*break tie, in sport*) they will play off next week

play on **1** *vi* (*continue to play*) the orchestra played on despite the bombardment; **2** *vipo* (*exploit*) he's just playing on your kindness with all those hard luck stories

play out *vtsep* **(a)** (*act*) that was quite a scene they played out for our benefit; **(b)** *usually in passive* (*be exhausted*) he's played out as a world class boxer; I feel quite played out; **(c)** (*accompany with music while leaving*) the organist played the congregation out

play up **1** *vi Fam* **(a)** (*cause difficulties*) the car is playing up again; **(b)** (*flatter*) he plays up to anyone who can further his career; **2** *vtas* (*cause difficulties for*) the baby has been playing me up all day

plough back *vtsep* (*re-invest, referring to money*) all the profits are ploughed back into the company

plug in **1** *vtsep* (*connect to electrical system*) plug the iron in; **2** *vi* (*put plug in socket*) it would help if you plugged in first!

plug up *vtsep* (*fill*) that gap will have to be plugged up

plump for *vipo Fam* (*decide or select after consideration*) I see you plumped for a car instead of a holiday

point out *vtsep* **(a)** (*identify*) can you point him out?; **(b)** (*specify*) she pointed out the extra work that this would entail

point up *vtsep* (*highlight*) why point up the difficulties?

poke about/around 1 *vi* (**a**) (*search*) poke about and see what you can find; the dog was poking about in the bushes; (**b**) (*make unwanted enquiries*) that social worker is always poking about; 2 *vipo* (*search in hope of finding something interesting*) I love poking about antique shops

poke out 1 *vi* (*protrude*) the label on your coat is poking out; 2 *vtsep* (**a**) (*push out*) she opened the window and poked her head out; (**b**) (*remove by poking*) careful or you'll poke my eye out!

polish off *vtsep Fam* (*eat, beat etc completely*) you polished that plate of pasta off in record time!; the sports commentators feel that he will polish this opponent off too

polish up *vtsep* (**a**) (*polish thoroughly*) the silver needs to be polished up; (**b**) (*improve*) I'm going to evening classes to polish up my maths

pop off *vi* (**a**) *Fam* (*die suddenly*) guess who popped off last night?; (**b**) (*go away quickly*) they're popping off for the weekend

pore over *vipo* (*examine closely*) he spends all his time poring over old manuscripts

pour out 1 *vi* (*leave in a flow*) smoke was pouring out of the windows; once she had composed herself, the words just poured out; 2 *vtsep* (**a**) (*put liquids or certain solids in container*) will I pour out the tea?; pour some sugar out into a bowl; (**b**) (*be profuse in expressing feelings etc*) I hope you didn't mind me pouring my troubles out like that

print out *vtsep* (*produce copy on a printer*) the text is edited on screen and then printed out to be sent back to the author

prop up *vtsep* (*support*) they've had to prop the castle walls up; the regime is being propped up by the military; *Humorous* you can usually find him propping up the bar at his local; (*lean*) he propped himself up against the gate

pull away 1 *vtsep* (*remove with some force*) they had to pull the distraught father away from the burning car; 2 *vi* (**a**) (*leave, of vehicle*) the train slowly pulled away; (**b**) (*retreat, of person or animal*) the dog pulled away when I tried to pat it; why do you keep pulling away?; (**c**) (*in race, increase lead*) she's beginning to pull away

pull down *vtsep* (**a**) (*lower*) pull the blind down; (**b**) (*demolish*) how many more buildings are they going to pull down?; (**c**) (*weaken*) this cold is really pulling me down; (**d**) *Am Fam* (*earn*) considering his qualifications, he doesn't pull down much of a salary

pull in 1 *vtsep* (**a**) (*attract*) the play is pulling people in by the coach-load; (**b**) (*arrest*) the police pulled him in for questioning; 2 *vi* (**a**) (*move to side of road and stop, of vehicle*) pull in here; (**b**) (*turn into*) we'll pull in to the next garage we see; (**c**) (*arrive, of train, bus etc*) the express pulled in two hours late

pull off *vtsep* (**a**) (**remove by pulling*) when I had pulled the paper off . . .; he pulled off his clothes; (**b**) (*succeed*) I never thought we would pull it off; he has pulled off a remarkable achievement

pull out 1 *vtsep* (**a**) (*extract*) he's having a tooth pulled out tomorrow; I'm stuck in this mud – you'll have to pull me out; (**b**) (*withdraw*) the president has promised that all troops will be pulled out by the end of the year; 2 *vi* (**a**) (*move out in order to overtake*) look in your mirror before you pull out; (**b**) (*depart, of train, bus*) when do we pull out?; (**c**) (*withdraw*) troops have begun to pull out

pull over 1 *vtsep* **(a)** (**put on, by pulling*) he pulled his sweater over his head; **(b)** (*cause to fall*) be careful or you'll pull the filing cabinet over on top of you; **2** *vi* (*move to one side*) the policeman asked us to pull over (*when driving*); she's pulling over to let the other runners past

pull through 1 *vtas* (*help someone to cope with, recover from illness, ordeal etc*) he says it was his faith that pulled him through; **2** *vi* (*recover*) I think we can confidently say that she will pull through

pull together 1 *vi* (*co-operate*) we must pull together on this; **2** *vtas* (*become calm, more organized*) come on, pull yourself together, there's a lot to be done

pull up 1 *vtsep* **(a)** (*bring or raise by pulling*) he pulled up a chair and joined us; pull the blind up; **(b)** (*reprimand*) she pulled him up about his bad language; the police pulled him up for not having his lights on; **2** *vi* **(a)** (*stop*) why are you pulling up?; the horse pulled up lame; **(b)** (*close gap*) he is beginning to pull up, but I think he's left it too late

push ahead *vi* **(a)** (*advance*) research on this is pushing ahead in various countries; **(b)** (*continue despite obstacles/problems*) I think we should push ahead nonetheless

push along 1 *vtsep* (*move by pushing*) as she pushed the pram along . . .; **2** *vi Fam* (*leave*) I suppose I should be pushing along soon

push around *vtsep Fam* (*bully*) I'm not going to let him push us around like this

push for *vipo* (*exerting pressure to obtain*) the company is pushing for more government funding

push off 1 *vtsep* (**remove by pushing*) push the lid off; **2** *vi* **(a)** (*go away*) everyone's pushing off at five o'clock; I wish you would push off and let me finish what I'm doing; **(b)** (*leave, of small boat*) we pushed off in the early hours of the morning

push on 1 *vi* (*continue with work, walk etc*) we decided to push on; **2** *vtsep* **(a)** (*apply pressure to*) I had to push it on to make it fit; **(b)** (*encourage*) both runners are being pushed on by the crowd

push through 1 *vipo* (*shove through*) we'll have to push through the crowd; **2** *vtsep** (*force acceptance of*) the government is pushing this bill through

push up *vtsep* **(a)** (*lift by pushing*) push up the window and let some air in; **(b)** (*increase*) excessive wage increases are pushing up inflation

put about *vtsep* (*spread, referring to gossip, news etc*) who put that rumour about?; it's being put about that . . .

put across *vtsep* **(a)** (*communicate, referring to joke, feelings etc*) he didn't put that across very well; she certainly knows how to put her ideas across; **(b)** (*set phrase*) to put one across somebody (*play joke on them*)

put away *vtsep* **(a)** (*return to pocket, container etc*) put your wallet away – I'm paying for this; could someone put the car away for the night?; **(b)** (*save money*) she puts something away every month for the proverbial rainy day; **(c)** (*consume food or especially alcohol*) this family puts away so much meat that I'm the butcher's favourite customer; he's down at the pub every night putting it away; you're putting it away a bit, aren't you?; **(d)** (*lock up in prison or mental institution*) that maniac should be put away somewhere

put back *vtsep* **(a)** (*restore to position*) put that back where you found it; **(b)** (*postpone*) the meeting's been put back till next month; **(c)** (*change time shown on clocks*) isn't this the week we put the clocks back?

put down *vtsep* **(a)** (*set down*) put that down before you drop it; **(b)** (*allow to get out of vehicle*) if you put me down at the next corner, I can walk the rest of the way; **(c)** (*land aircraft*) you'll have to put her down on the motorway; **(d)** (*suppress*) we will put this uprising down with the utmost firmness; **(e)** *Fam* (*say negative things about*) he's always putting her down; why do you keep putting yourself down?; **(f)** (*kill pet for humane reasons*) the cat's in a great deal of pain – I think we should have her put down; **(g)** (*pay*) how much do you have to put down as a deposit?; **(h)** (*write*) have you put all the details down?; **(i)** (*attribute to a cause*) she puts it down to laziness

put forward *vtsep* **(a)** (*suggest*) somebody put forward the rather good idea that . . .; they've put him forward for a knighthood; **(b)** (*advance date or time*) the meeting has been put forward to noon today

put in **1** *vtsep* **(a)** (*place in*) have you put everything in?; **(b)** (*install*) we're finally having a telephone put in; **(c)** (*spend time doing*) I put in a lot of overtime last month; don't you think you should put in a bit of piano practice?; **2** *vtas* (*enter*) we're putting him in for the 500 and 1000 metres; **3** *vi* (*apply*) has he put in for that job we saw advertised?

put off **1** *vtsep* **(a)** (**allow to get off vehicle*) could you put me off at the High Street?; **(b)** (**force to get off vehicle*) the bus conductor put the boys off because of their behaviour; **(c)** (*postpone*) let's put lunch off to another time; **(d)** (*make excuses to*) you can't keep putting him off like this – just tell him you don't want to go out with him; **(e)** (*referring to electrical equipment, stop*) put the TV off; **2** *vtas* **(a)** (*create dislike in*) their stories have put me off foreign travel; that programme on slaughter houses put him off meat for a week; **(b)** (*disturb*) you would think that all those people standing round watching would put her off

put on **1** *vtsep* **(a)** (**put on oneself, referring to clothes etc*) put your coat on; she put on her glasses; **(b)** (*act, not be truthful*) the boss can put on a show of being fierce; she puts on a posh accent sometimes; he's just putting it on; **(c)** (*produce programme, play etc*) they're not putting Hamlet on again?; why can't they put on something decent on TV for a change?; **(d)** (*add to weight, price etc*) he's put on a few inches round the waist; **(e)** (*referring to electrical equipment, start*) put the radio on; **2** *vtas* (*change time shown on clock etc*) we had to put our watches on several times when we flew to Australia

put on to *vtaspo* (*provide information about*) I can put you on to an excellent restaurant; what put the police on to him as the culprit?

put out **1** *vtsep* **(a)** (*place outside*) don't forget to put the milk bottles out; **(b)** (*arrange for use*) have you put the side plates out as well?; **(c)** (*extend*) she put her hand out; **(d)** (*issue*) we'll be putting out a new edition very soon; **(e)** (*extinguish*) put the light out; **(f)** (*make unconscious, referring to patient etc*) the drug will put you out very quickly; **2** *vtas* **(a)** (*make cross*) everyone was put out by the two hour delay; **(b)** (*inconvenience*) would one more guest put you out?; I don't want to put anyone out; **(c)** (*dislocate, referring to shoulder etc*) don't lift that table or you'll put your back out again

put through 1 *vtsep* **(a)** (**accept*) a bill has been put through Parliament that . . .; **(b)** (*connect by telephone*) will you put me through to the book department, please?; **2** *vtaspo* (*cause to suffer*) you've put your mother through a great deal of anxiety with your behaviour

put up *vtsep* **(a)** (*raise*) put up your hand if you know the answer; **(b)** (*erect*) a new block of flats is being put up just behind their house; **(c)** (*fasten to wall*) I want to put up a few more pictures in this room; **(d)** (*increase*) car manufacturers are putting their prices up again; **(e)** (*provide accommodation for*) could you put us up while we're in town?; **(f)** (*offer*) a lot of people have put their houses up for sale; she put up a good fight but had to concede defeat in the end

put up with *vipo* (*tolerate*) why do you put up with that kind of behaviour?; it's a lot to have to put up with

Q

quieten down 1 *vi* **(a)** (*become quiet*) if you lot don't quieten down I'm going to get very cross; **(b)** (*become calm*) business always quietens down after Christmas; **2** *vtsep* **(a)** (*make quiet*) it took me ages to quieten the class down; **(b)** (*make calm*) the nurse tried to quieten the child down but he kept crying for his mother

R

rain off (*Am* = **rain out**) *vtsep usually passive* (*cancel because of rain*) the match was rained off

rattle through *vipo* **(a)** (*move with rattling noise*) the two old cars rattled through the streets; **(b)** (*do or say something quickly*) she tends to rattle through her work; the speaker fairly rattled through his speech

read out *vtsep* (*say aloud*) he read out the names of the injured

read up on *vipo* (*study, with implication that not much is known about subject*) the play might have been more meaningful if you'd read up a bit on the events it depicted

rein in **1** *vtsep* **(a)** (*slow by pulling on reins*) the girl reined her pony in and turned back towards the stables; **(b)** (*restrain*) he tried very hard to rein his anger in; the council wants to rein in its spending on sports facilities; **2** *vi* **(a)** (*slow horse*) they reined in so they could talk; **(b)** (*restrain spending*) we'll have to rein in this month

rest up *vi* (*rest*) the doctor has told him to rest up

ring back *vi Br* (*telephone again*) could you ring back in half an hour?

ring in *vi Br* (*report by telephone*) you ought to have rung in to say you were ill and couldn't come to work

ring off *vi Br* (*end telephone call*) I must ring off now, there's someone at the door

ring out *vi* (*be loud and clear*) her voice rang out; the church bells were ringing out

ring up *vtsep Br* (*contact by telephone*) why not ring her up and ask?

rip off *vtsep* **(a)** (**remove quickly by pulling*) as soon as they got their hands on the presents, the children ripped the paper off; **(b)** *Sl* (*cheat by charging too much*) let's choose another restaurant – I was ripped off the last time I was at this one

rip up *vtsep* (*tear into small pieces*) just rip his letter up and forget the whole business

root for *vipo* (*support in a contest*) which side are you rooting for?; the candidate I root for invariably loses

rough out *vtsep* (*make outline or draft of*) could you rough out a publicity campaign?

rough up *vtsep* **(a)** (*ruffle*) don't rough up my hair; **(b)** (*attack physically*) he was roughed up by some soccer fans; they roughed her up a bit but she's all right

round down *vtsep* (*reduce to nearest whole number*) the price will be rounded down

round off *vtsep* **(a)** (*make smooth*) round off the edges; **(b)** (*end*) we rounded the meal off with coffee and liqueurs; she rounded off her presentation by saying . . .

round on *vipo* (*attack verbally or physically*) rounding on his tormentors, he shouted . . .

round up *vtsep* **(a)** (*collect in a group*) about this time of year the cattle are rounded up; round everyone up for the meeting, will you?; **(b)** (*increase to nearest whole number*) just round the bill up to 50

rub down *vtsep* (*dry*) the groom will rub your horse down; he rubbed himself down with the towel

rub in *vtsep* **(a)** (*put on lotion, suntan oil etc*) rub the cream in well; **(b)** *Fam* (*emphasize, with negative connotations*) she kept rubbing in his unpunctuality; I know I was wrong – don't keep rubbing it in!

rub off **1** *vtsep** (*remove by rubbing*) rub these dirty marks off the wall; the teacher rubbed the equations off the blackboard; **2** *vi* **(a)** (*be removed by rubbing*) the stain won't rub off; **(b)** *Fig* (*referring to good or bad qualities, be acquired through contact*) I hope his attitude to authority doesn't rub off on you

rub out *vtsep* **(a)** (*remove by rubbing*) try rubbing the stain out with soap and water; **(b)** (*remove with eraser*) don't rub out your calculations; **(c)** *Sl* (*kill*) the gang decided to rub the witness out before she could talk to police

run about **1** *vipo* (*move about in a busy way*) I refuse to run about the shops looking for presents for people I don't like; **2** *vi* (*be very busy*) she's been running about all day preparing for her mother-in-law's visit

run across *vipo* (*meet by chance*) if you should run across John give him my regards; I've run across a word I don't know

run away with *vipo* **(a)** (*elope*) I know it sounds ridiculous, but his wife has run away with the milkman!; **(b)** (*flee*) the man in the butcher's has run away with the week's takings; **(c)** (*referring to imagination, enthusiasm etc, take control*) jogging five times a week is what I call letting your enthusiasm run away with you; if I'm not careful, she'll run away with the idea that I'm very easy-going (*ie will wrongly get that idea*); **(d)** (*use up, especially money*) repairs to the house have run away with most of our savings

run back **1** *vi* **(a)** (*return by running*) I ran back to the car; **(b)** (*return to wife or husband*) he'll come running back once he's had his fling; **2** *vtas* (*transport home by car*) don't worry about the last bus – I'll run you back

run down **1** *vi* **(a)** (*go down stairs running*) run down and see who's at the door; **(b)** (*lose power and stop working*) the government is accused of letting the industry run down; don't wind the clock until it has completely run down; you've let the battery run down; **2** *vtsep* **(a)** (*hit, referrring to a vehicle*) she was run down by a bus; **(b)** (*speak ill of*) you shouldn't run everyone down so; **(c)**

(*diminish*) remember to switch off the lights or they'll run the battery down; the factory is being deliberately run down; **(d)** (*find after much searching*) the police finally ran him down in Hove

run in 1 *vi* (*enter running*) she came running in to tell us; **2** *vtsep* **(a)** *Br* (*accustom to use*) it will be another couple of weeks before we've run the new machine in; **(b)** *Fam* (*arrest*) they ran him in for drunk driving

run into *vipo* **(a)** (*collide with*) he ran into an old lady as he ran for his train; **(b)** (*meet by chance*) guess who I ran into last week; **(c)** (*amount to*) the cost will run into millions

run off 1 *vi* (*go away*) I haven't seen next door's dog for ages – I hope he's run off; **2** *vtsep* **(a)** (*reproduce*) will you run off six copies of this?; **(b)** (*compose or write something quickly*) she runs these magazine articles off in her spare time; **(c)** (*get rid of something by running*) he's a bit overweight and wants to run off a few pounds

run out 1 *vi* (*come to an end*) your time is running out; **2** *vtsep* (*eliminate in cricket*) he was run out for ten

run out of *vipo* (*no longer have something desirable or necessary*) I have run out of patience with you; we're running out of butter; with two miles to go we ran out of petrol

run over 1 *vi* **(a)** (*visit quickly*) I won't be a minute – I'm just running over to the shops; **(b)** (*exceed allotted time*) television broadcasts of sports events often run over into the next programme; **(c)** (*overflow*) the sink is running over; **2** *vipo* (*examine, check*) the doctor will want to run over your case history; let's run over the arrangements one last time; **3** *vtas* (*transport by car*) I'm running Mum over to Grandad's – do you want to come?; **4** *vtsep* (*knock down with *vehicle*) he ran an old lady over

run through 1 *vipo* **(a)** (*use up*) I hate to think how many clean shirts he runs through in a week; **(b)** (*rehearse*) would you like me to run through your speech with you?; **2** *vtsep* (*pierce with sword*) the coachman ran the highwayman through

run up **1** *vi* **(a)** (*go upstairs running*) run up and fetch my purse for me; **(b)** (*arrive running*) people ran up to see if they could help; **2** *vtsep* **(a)** (*make quickly, referring to clothes*) the dressmaker said she could run the suit up for me in a couple of days; **(b)** (*incur*) you've run up a lot of bills this month; **(c)** (*hoist, referring to flags*) they run the flag up on special occasions

rush at *vi* **(a)** (*attack*) he rushed at the burglar; **(b)** (*tackle without thought*) it's not the kind of job that can be rushed at – take your time

rush through **1** *vtsep* **(a)** (*transport at speed*) the necessary equipment has been rushed through to the rescue workers; **(b)** (**process at speed*) could you rush my order through?; **2** *vtaspo* (*hurry someone*) they rushed us through Customs; you rushed me through lunch and now you're rushing me through dinner – what's the hurry?

rustle up *vtsep Fam* (*produce or make quickly, especially food or drink*) could you rustle up a meal for me?

S

save up **1** *vi* (*save, with a goal in mind*) if you want a new motor-bike you'll have to start saving up, won't you?; **2** *vtsep* **(a)** (*not spend*) you should save up part of your pocket money for Christmas presents; **(b)** (*accumulate*) one of the children's programmes on TV has asked viewers to save up silver paper

score off 1 *vtsep** (*delete*) score his name off the guest list; 2 *vipo* (*succeed in winning a point, especially in argument*) the speaker scored off the government when he reminded them of their campaign promises

score out *vtsep* (*put a line through*) score any mistakes out neatly

scrape along *vi* (*only just manage, especially financially*) she's scraping along until her next pay cheque

scrape by/through *vi* (*only just succeed, especially in exam*) I don't mind scraping by, as long as I pass

scrape together/up *vtsep* (*collect with considerable difficulty*) I'll scrape the money together for you somehow

scream out 1 *vi* (*emit a scream*) the pain made him scream out; 2 *vtsep* (*scream*) the sergeant major screamed out his orders

screw up *vtsep* **(a)** (*crush*) she screwed the letter up and threw it in the fire; **(b)** (*contort*) don't screw your face up like that; **(c)** (*spoil*) this rush job has screwed up my plans for the weekend; **(d)** (*mishandle*) you screwed the whole thing up – next time let me do the talking; **(e)** (*make neurotic*) he claims it was his parents that screwed him up; she's all screwed up that girl

see about *vipo* **(a)** (*attend to*) you'll have to see about those cracks in the ceiling; **(b)** (*consider*) I'll see about it; *Ironical* so they're going to win, are they? well, we'll see about that

see across *vtas* (*escort to other side*) she saw me across the road

see in 1 *vi* (*look in*) they always keep the curtains drawn so people can't see in ; 2 *vtsep* (*escort in*) always see guests in

see off *vtsep* (*say goodbye to at station, airport etc*) who's coming to see you off?

see out 1 *vi* (*look out*) another passenger changed seats with the little boy so he could see out; **2** *vtsep* **(a)** (*escort to door*) my husband will see you out, doctor; **(b)** (*last until the end of*) I don't think my boots will see the winter out

see over/round *vipo* (*tour, visit*) would you like to see over our new house?

see through 1 *vipo* (*not be deceived by*) why do you persist with these stories? – everyone can see through them; **2** *vtas* (*help to cope with*) friends and neighbours are seeing them through this bad time; a couple of hundred gallons of oil should see us through the winter

see to *vipo* (*deal with*) let your husband see to the baby – you relax for a bit

see up *vtsep* (*escort upstairs*) do you know where his room is or do you want me to see you up?

seize up *vi* (*not work, become stuck in one position*) if you don't put some oil in soon the engine will seize up; my knee always seizes up at the most inconvenient times

seize (up)on *vipo* (*grasp*) it seemed like an excellent idea and we seized on it immediately

sell off *vtsep* (*dispose of at low price*) the shoe shop is closing down soon and has started to sell off its stock

sell out **1** *vtsep* **(a)** (*sell all stocks of something*) how can a supermarket be sold out of butter?; **(b)** (*betray for money or other gain*) the rebel leaders were accused of selling their supporters out; **2** *vi* **(a)** (*sell all stocks*) all of the shops I tried had sold out; **(b)** (*sell a business*) they are selling out since they want to retire; **(c)** (*betray a cause, surrender*) we will negotiate but we will never sell out

sell up 1 *vtsep* (*force to sell*) something has to be done to prevent farmers being sold up and losing their livelihood; **2** *vi* (*sell because of necessity*) since she can no longer run the business on her own, she has decided to sell up

send away *vtsep* (*send to another place*) a boy of seven is too young to be sent away to school

send away for *vipo* (*write and request*) send away for your free gift now; you should send away for an application form

send down *vtsep* **(a)** (*send to lower place*) the people upstairs sent a lovely cake down for us; **(b)** (*cause to fall*) the rumours have sent share prices down; **(c)** *Br Fam* (*send to prison*) the judge sent her down for two years; **(d)** *Br* (*expel from university*) all of the students involved in the incident were sent down for a term

send for *vipo* (*summon*) I think we should send for the doctor

send in *vtsep* (*send to a place*) send Mr Martin in as soon as he arrives please; a lot of viewers have sent in comments on the programme we aired last week

send off *vtsep* **(a)** (*send by post to a place*) have you sent that letter off yet?; **(b)** (*in football etc, order player to leave match temporarily for bad behaviour*) he was sent off for spitting at the referee

send on *vtsep* **(a)** (*forward*) would you send on any letters that come for me?; **(b)** (*send in advance when travelling*) we've decided to send our luggage on so we don't have as much to carry

send out *vtsep* **(a)** (*ask or order to leave*) the teacher sent him out of the classroom for talking; **(b)** (*send to find*) I've forgotten to buy milk but I'll send one of the kids out for it; **(c)** (*emit*) the satellite has stopped sending out signals; **(d)** (*send by post to *a person*) those invitations should have been sent out a week ago

send out for 1 *vipo* (*have food or drink delivered*) do you want to send out for a sandwich?; 2 *vtaspo* (*send someone to buy*) send the office junior out for coffee

send up *vtsep* **(a)** (*release into sky*) the crew sent up a distress rocket; **(b)** (*cause to rise*) news of the takeover bid sent up the company's share prices; **(c)** (*make fun of*) politicians are very easy to send up; don't you know when you're being sent up?; **(d)** *Am Fam* (*send to prison*) he was sent up for armed robbery

serve out *vtsep* **(a)** (*distribute something to a lot of people*) the soup kitchen needs volunteers to serve food out; **(b)** (*work until end of*) Dad had only just served out his apprenticeship when the war started

set about *vipo* **(a)** (*start, especially something considered as work*) she set about the washing up; **(b)** (*tackle*) be sure to take expert advice before you set about rewiring the house; **(c)** (*attack physically or verbally*) the old lady set about the boys with her stick; Mum set about me for leaving my room in such a mess

set against *vtaspo* **(a)** (*cause to oppose*) something must have set him against the idea; it was her friends who set her against me; **(b)** (*use to reduce financial obligation*) some expenses can be set against taxes; **(c)** (*look at in the light of*) we must set the government's promises against its performance in the past

set apart *vtsep* (*distinguish*) what sets her apart from all the other children in my class is . . .

set aside *vtsep* **(a)** (*abandon temporarily*) could you set aside what you're working on and do this instead?; **(b)** (*save*) I've decided to set aside some money every week; **(c)** (*not consider*) setting that particular aspect of the issue aside, . . .; **(d)** (*in law, cancel decision taken by lower court*) the Supreme Court has set aside the decision

set back *vtsep* **(a)** (*place at distance*) the cottage is set back quite a bit from the road; **(b)** (*delay*) the strike has set the company back at least a month in its deliveries; **(c)** *Fam* (*cost*) that new car must have set him back a bit; will it set me back more than a thousand?

set down *vtsep* **(a)** (*put down, often something heavy*) you can set those cases down in the hall; **(b)** (*allow to alight from vehicle*) the bus stopped to set down one or two passengers; **(c)** (*state what is required, referring to laws etc*) *usually in passive* permissible levels of pollution are set down in the regulations; **(d)** (*record in writing*) the policeman set down the details in his notebook

set forth *vtsep* (*present*) would you like to set forth your suggestions to the committee?; this document sets forth a detailed description of . . .

set in *vi* (*begin, referring to disease, weather etc*) the doctors are worried that gangrene might set in; winter seems to be setting in early this year

set off **1** *vtsep* **(a)** (*detonate*) terrorists have set off yet another bomb in a crowded street; **(b)** (*cause*) what set the argument off?; **(c)** (*cause to laugh, cry etc*) that last joke of his set us all off; if you say any more you'll only set her off again; he is so allergic to pollen that even a vase of cut flowers sets him off; **(d)** (*enhance*) those velvet curtains really set the room off; **(e)** (*balance against*) can I set these expenses off against my tax liability?; **2** *vi* (*depart*) we'll have to set off at dawn

set on 1 *vtaspo* **(a)** (*cause to attack*) if you don't get off my land immediately, I'll set the dogs on you; **2** *vipo* (*attack*) travellers were often set on by highwaymen

set out 1 *vtsep* **(a)** (*arrange*) the desserts were set out on a trolley in an eye-catching display; **(b)** (*state*) this document sets out the steps that must be taken; **2** *vi* **(a)** (*depart on journey*) they set out late last night; **(b)** (*start*) I didn't realize when I set out just how long the job was going to take me; **(c)** (*do something with intent*) don't set out to annoy me

set to 1 *vi* (*start working*) isn't it about time that we set to and cleaned out the garage?; **2** *vipo* (*start doing*) when are the builders going to set to work?

set up 1 *vi* **(a)** (*establish oneself*) they've decided to set up in business for themselves; she's setting up as a hairdresser; **(b)** (*claim oneself to be*) he sets himself up as a poet; **2** *vtsep* **(a)** (*erect*) marquees will be set up on the front lawn; **(b)** (*arrange*) I'd like to set up an appointment with the doctor; **(c)** (*establish*) he's set her up in a flat of her own; a task force will be set up to investigate the matter; **(d)** (*cause*) these pills won't set up a reaction, will they?; **(e)** *Fam* (*fabricate evidence against*) *usually passive* there's no point in claiming you were set up – no-one will believe you

settle down 1 *vi* **(a)** (*make oneself comfortable*) I had just settled down with a book when the phone rang; **(b)** (*become calm*) now settle down, children; **(c)** (*give serious attention*) he must settle down to his homework; **(d)** (*have permanent home, job etc*) when are you going to settle down and get married?; **2** *vtsep* **(a)** (*make comfortable*) just let me settle the baby down for the night; **(b)** (*make calm*) I couldn't settle my class down at all today

settle for *vipo* (*accept as substitute*) we haven't got any brandy I'm afraid – will you settle for Scotch?; is that a fixed price for the house or would the seller settle for less?

settle in **1** *vi* (*become established*) how are you settling in in the new house?; he'll soon settle in at the job; **2** *vtsep** (*help to become established*) I'm just going to settle the new secretary in and then I'm having a holiday; do you want us to come over and help settle you in?

settle on *vipo* (*decide something after thought, discussion*) have you settled on a date for the wedding yet?

settle up *vi* **(a)** (*pay bill, especially in restaurant*) can I leave you to settle up?; **(b)** (*pay debt*) he said he would settle up with us later

shake off *vtsep* **(a)** (**remove by shaking*) shake the snow off your coat before you come in; **(b)** (*get rid of, referring to illness, bad mood etc*) I can't seem to shake this cold off; **(c)** (*escape from*) she shook the detective off by going into the ladies and leaving by a back door

shake up *vtsep* **(a)** (*mix by shaking*) shake it up a bit – all the solids are at the bottom; don't shake the champagne up; **(b)** (*make plump, referring to cushions etc*) let me shake your pillows up for you; **(c)** (*upset*) the news of the accident shook her up; I was badly shaken up by my narrow escape; **(d)** (*make changes in something, the implication being that it is old fashioned*) this committee needs shaking up a bit; this will shake their ideas up

shell out *vtsep Fam* (*pay, especially unwillingly*) I'm not going to shell out any more on that motor bike of his; how much do we each have to shell out for petrol?

shoot down *vtsep* **(a)** (*bring aircraft down by gunfire, missile*) he was shot down over France; the guerrillas claim to have shot down three planes in the last week; **(b)** *Fam* (*show to be wrong or unacceptable*) she shot his argument down; if he doesn't like your proposal he'll shoot it down

shoot out **1** *vi* (*emerge quickly*) bulbs are shooting out all over the garden; **2** *vtsep* (*put out quickly*) she shot out her hand and grabbed him before he could fall

shoot up **1** *vi* (*rise quickly*) house prices have shot up in the last year; hands were shooting up all over the room to ask questions; **2** *vtsep* (*damage by gunfire*) the runways are so badly shot up that they are unuseable

shop around *vi* (*compare prices and quality of goods before buying*) it pays to shop around

shout down *vtsep* (*express disapproval of by shouting*) union members shouted down management's proposal; don't shout her down – listen to what she has to say

show off **1** *vi* (*try to gain admiration through one's behaviour*) he was flexing his muscles and generally showing off; **2** *vtsep* **(a)** (*flaunt*) I think I'll go for a drive round town and show the new car off; **(b)** (*highlight*) wearing white always shows off a tan

show up **1** *vi* **(a)** (*be evident*) the dirt really shows up on a pale carpet; **(b)** *Fam* (*arrive*) he showed up wearing a new suit; she's always showing up late; **2** *vtsep* **(a)** (*highlight, especially in negative sense*) the loss of export markets shows up the company's failure to modernize; **(b)** *Fam* (*shame*) I don't want you showing me up in front of people, so don't tell any of your crude jokes; **(c)** (*escort upstairs*) the porter will show you up to your room

shrug off *vtsep* (*treat as unimportant*) he shrugs off all criticism

shut away *vtsep* (*keep apart from people*) he's been shut away in prison for the last year; ever since her husband's death, she has shut herself away

shut down *vtsep* and *vi* = **close down**

shut in *vtsep** (*confine in a place*) shut the dog in the kitchen

shut off **1** *vtsep* **(a)** (*stop a machine etc*) will I shut the television off?; **(b)** (*isolate*) don't they feel shut off living in the depths of the countryside?; **2** *vi* (*stop functioning*) I want a kettle that shuts off automatically

shut out *vtsep* **(a)** (*not allow to enter*) the door's locked – they've shut us out; I've forgotten my key and now I'm shut out; **(b)** *Fig* (*exclude*) people want to help – why do you insist on shutting them out?; **(c)** (*hide*) we're going to plant some trees to shut out the view of the railway line

shut up **1** *vtsep* **(a)** (*confine*) shut the cat up somewhere – you know Mrs Williams is allergic; **(b)** (*close for a period of time*) they're away shutting up their cottage for the winter; **(c)** *Fam* (*make quiet*) shut those kids up – I'm trying to concentrate; **2** *vi Fam* (*stop talking*) don't tell me to shut up!

shy away *vi* (*retreat in fear or nervousness*) she shied away when he tried to put his arm around her

shy away from *vipo* (*avoid because of fear or nervousness*) he has shied away from driving ever since the accident

sift out *vtsep* **(a)** (*remove by sifting*) sift out any impurities; **(b)** (*eliminate*) we have sifted out the most obviously unsuitable candidates

sign away *vtsep* (*concede by signing*) read the small print to be sure you're not signing away any of your rights

sign for *vipo* (*acknowledge receipt of by signing*) there's a registered letter for you – will you sign for it please?

sign in **1** *vi* (*gain entrance by signing*) it's a rule of the club that all visitors must sign in; **2** *vtsep* (*gain entrance for someone by signing*) I'm a member, so I can sign you in

sign off *vi* **(a)** (*stop broadcasting*) they usually sign off for the day at midnight; he always signs off with that catch phrase; **(b)** *Fam* (*phrase used to end letter*) I think I'll sign off now and go to bed

sign on *vi Br* (*register for unemployment benefit*) how long do you have to be out of work before you can sign on?; I have to sign on every Monday

sign up **1** *vtsep* (*enlist*) the committee wants to sign up more volunteers to help with the fund drive; **2** *vi* **(a)** (*enlist*) my uncle tried to sign up when he was only 15; **(b)** (*register, especially for course*) she has signed up for a class in car maintenance

simmer down *vi* (*become calmer*) I'll tell you what he said once I've simmered down

single out *vtsep* (*choose one from many*) why single her out for praise – we all contributed to the success of the project

sink in *vi* **(a)** (*be absorbed*) pour the syrup over the cake and allow it to sink in; **(b)** (*be understood*) his remark didn't sink in until she was halfway down the stairs

sit about/around *vi* (*be idle*) we had to sit about the airport lounge for two hours

sit back *vi* **(a)** (*make oneself comfortable*) now sit back and watch the next episode of our thriller; **(b)** (*not take action*) we can't just sit back if we think something's wrong next door

sit down 1 *vi* (*be seated*) you'd better sit down – I've got some bad news; **2** *vtas* (*tell to be seated*) the doctor sat her down and explained the operation

sit in *vi* **(a)** (*occupy, referring to university etc*) students used to sit in regularly in the sixties; **(b)** (*act as substitute*) the chairwoman is ill and has asked me to sit in for her at the meeting

sit on *vipo* **(a)** (*be member of*) how many people sit on the committee?; **(b)** (*conceal*) reporters were asked to sit on the news until the hostages were safely out of the country; **(c)** (*not take action on*) the company decided to sit on the consultant's recommendations; **(d)** *Fam* (*silence with some force*) I'm sorry I had to sit on you like that but you were about to be indiscreet

sit out *vtsep* **(a)** (*not dance*) I'd rather sit this one out; **(b)** (*endure without action*) we sat the concert out to the bitter end but it didn't get any better

sit up 1 *vi* **(a)** (*be upright*) she was sitting up in bed when I arrived; sit up straight for goodness sake and don't slouch!; **(b)** (*rise to sitting position*) sit up – I've brought you breakfast in bed; **(c)** (*not go to bed*) we sat up until midnight waiting for them to arrive; **2** *vtas* (*raise to sitting position*) the nurse sat the old man up

size up *vtsep Fam* (*form opinion of*) she looked round the room, sizing everyone up

skim off *vtsep** (*remove top layer, often Fig*) he always skims off the best applicants for his department

skim over/through *vipo* (*read very quickly to extract most important parts*) the lawyer skimmed over his client's statement

slap on *vtsep* Fam* **(a)** (*apply quickly and carelessly*) just slap some paint on and that will hide the marks; **(b)** (*add*) I bet the government slaps some more on the cost of a pint in the next budget

sleep around *vi Fam* (*be promiscuous*) Aids has stopped people sleeping around

sleep in *vi* **(a)** *Fam* (*sleep late*) I always sleep in on Sunday; **(b)** (*live at place of work*) she has two maids sleeping in

sleep off *vtsep* (*get rid of something by sleeping*) he's upstairs sleeping his hangover off

sleep on **1** *vi* (*continue sleeping*) let her sleep on for as long as she likes; **2** *vipo* (*postpone decision until next day*) you don't have to make your mind up now – sleep on it and then call me

sleep together *vi* (*have sexual relationship*) when did you start to sleep together?

sleep with *vipo* (*have sexual relationship with*) she's been sleeping with him for a year

slip away *vi* (*escape, elapse etc quietly, without being noticed*) she slipped away from the party; the time just slips away when I'm with him

slip by **1** *vi* (*pass quickly*) the time has slipped by; **2** *vipo* (*escape attention of*) how did that mistake manage to slip by you?

slip in **1** *vi* (*enter quietly etc*) he slipped in to the room; **2** *vtsep* (*insert in a quiet way*) she slipped in a remark about . . .

slip off **1** *vi* (*leave quietly etc*) we didn't see you go – when did you slip off?; **2** *vtsep* (*remove quickly*) she slipped off her coat

slip on *vtsep* (*put on quickly*) she slipped a dress on and ran to answer the door

slip out *vi* **(a)** (*leave quietly etc*) we slipped out halfway through the concert; **(b)** (*escape, especially of tactless remarks etc*) she's very apologetic about giving the secret away – it just slipped out when she was talking to him

slip up *vi Fam* (*make mistake*) slip up one more time and you're fired

slow down **1** *vi* **(a)** (*make vehicle go more slowly*) slow down – there's a speed limit here; **(b)** (*talk, work, walk etc more slowly*) slow down – I can't understand what you're saying; **2** *vtsep* (*cause to go more slowly*) can't you walk any faster? you're slowing everyone down

smooth down *vtsep* **(a)** (*make smooth*) the duck smoothed down her ruffled feathers; **(b)** (*calm tension or anger*) he's really very upset – give me a few minutes to smooth him down

smooth out *vtsep* **(a)** (*make smooth*) she smoothed out the creases from the tablecloth; **(b)** (*resolve, especially difficulty*) we have a little problem we hope you can help us smooth out

smooth over *vtsep* (*make difficulty etc seem trivial*) the chairman smoothed over the dispute with a light remark

snap out *vtsep* (*say sharply*) the sergeant snapped out an order

snap out of *vipo* (*emerge from feeling, mood etc quickly*) you must snap out of this depression

snap up *vtsep Fam* (*buy quickly*) the towels are so cheap people are snapping them up

snarl up *vtsep* (*confuse, especially traffic*) because of the accident, traffic is all snarled up on the motorway

snow under *vtas Fam usually passive* (*bury*) we have been snowed under with requests for a repeat of the programme about bird migration

soldier on *vi* (*persevere*) I know you're all very tired but if you could soldier on till the project is finished, I'd be very grateful

sort out *vtsep* **(a)** (*arrange*) I've sorted out all those tools that you had just thrown in the drawer; **(b)** (*select*) the women on the production line sort out the flawed goods with incredible speed; **(c)** (*solve*) maybe he needs some psychiatric help to sort out his problems; **(d)** *Sl* (*deal with verbally or physically, implying that someone is being a problem*) it's about time someone sorted him out

sound off *vi* (*express opinions forcefully, especially as a complaint*) she is always sounding off about rude shop assistants

sound out *vtsep* (*check opinion of*) I want to recommend you for the job but I thought I should sound you out first and see if you'd be interested

spell out *vtsep* **(a)** (*spell aloud*) it's rather an unusual name so I'll spell it out for you; **(b)** (*describe in detail*) the chairman spelled out what a strike would mean for the company's future; do I have to spell it out for you?

spin out *vtsep* **(a)** (*make last something of which there is not very much*) can you spin the housekeeping money out until the end of the month?; **(b)** (*prolong*) I'd like to spin my leave out for another couple of days

splash down *vi* (*return to earth, landing in the water, referring to spacecraft*) the capsule splashed down at 13.00 hours just off Haiti

splash out *vi Fam* (*spend a lot*) let's splash out for once and stay in the best hotels

split up **1** *vtsep* (*divide*) we're going to split the money up among our children; **2** *vi* (*separate, referring to couple*) I hear they're splitting up

spring up *vi* (*appear suddenly*) weeds are springing up all over the garden after the rain; the company sprang up almost overnight

square up *vi* **(a)** (*settle debts*) can we square up later?; I'll square up with you when I get paid if that's all right; **(b)** (*assume fighting position*) the two men were so angry with each other they began to square up; **(c)** (*face difficulty etc with determination*) it was wonderful the way you squared up to that bully

stamp out *vtsep* (*eradicate*) the military government has vowed to stamp out unrest

stand by **1** *vi* **(a)** (*not be involved*) people just stood by and watched the policeman being beaten up; **(b)** (*wait*) viewers were told to stand by for further developments; **2** *vipo* (*keep, honour*) the government has promised to stand by its election promises

stand down *vi* (*retire, especially from office*) he will stand down as chairman of the football club at the end of the year

stand for *vipo* **(a)** (*present oneself as candidate for office*) she is standing for election; I have decided to stand for the chairmanship of the committee; **(b)** (*mean, represent*) in a recipe, "tsp" stands for teaspoonful; **(c)** (*tolerate*) I won't stand for that kind of behaviour

stand in *vi* (*act as replacement*) Mr Wilson has very kindly agreed to stand in at short notice for our scheduled speaker

stand out *vi* **(a)** (*be noticeable*) he is so tall that he stands out in a crowd; what makes her stand out is . . .; **(b)** (*adopt firm position for or against*) we are standing out against management's attempts to break our strike

stand up 1 *vi* (**a**) (*rise to one's feet*) everyone stood up when the president entered the room; (**b**) (*be valid, referring to argument etc*) the prosecution hasn't got enough evidence for the charge to stand up; **2** *vtsep* (*fail to meet as arranged, especially boyfriend or girlfriend*) poor old Tom – that's the second time this month she's stood him up

stand up for *vipo* (*support, defend especially in difficult situation*) my parents stood up for me when I was in trouble; stand up for what you believe in

stand up to *vipo* (*confront*) I admired the way she stood up to that aggressive drunk

start off 1 *vi* (*begin journey etc*) the runners will be starting off in the coolness of the early morning; to put your audience at ease, start off with a joke or two; **2** *vtsep* (**a**) (*begin*) start your presentation off with a brief history of the problem; (**b**) (*cause someone to start doing*) there's the baby crying again – what started her off this time?

start up 1 *vi* (**a**) (*start functioning, referring to machine etc*) she heard a car starting up next door; (**b**) (*begin, referring to business etc*) there's a new dry cleaner's starting up on the corner; **2** *vtsep* (**a**) (*cause to function*) start the engines up; (**b**) (*begin, referring to business etc*) they're starting up another restaurant

stay off 1 *vi* (**a**) (*not go to work, school*) he's decided to stay off and see if he can cure this cold; (**b**) (*not begin, referring to bad weather*) do you think the rain will stay off until the washing's dry?; **2** *vipo* (*not attend*) can I stay off school today?

stay out *vi* (**a**) (*not come home*) what do you mean by staying out until this time of night?; (**b**) (*continue* *strike*) the women have decided to stay out until their demands are met

step in *vi* (*intervene*) the government should step in and order the strikers back to work

step up *vtsep* (*accelerate, increase*) research into this disease must be stepped up; the company is stepping up production of the vaccine

stick around *vi Fam* (*not go away*) stick around, we may need you

stick out **1** *vi* **(a)** (*protrude*) his ears stick out; **(b)** (*be noticeable*) it's the way she dresses that makes her stick out; **2** *vtsep* (*put out*) stick your head out the window and see if they're coming

stick to *vipo* **(a)** (*adhere to*) the cloth is sticking to the table; **(b)** (*not give up, stay with*) she's sticking to her plans despite her parents' opposition; if red wine gives you a headache, stick to white; **(c)** (*continue with to end*) it's a very tough programme of work – do you think you'll stick to it?

stop by *vi* (*visit briefly*) stop by at the post office on your way home; we'll stop by and see you next week

stop off *vi* (*stay briefly*) they're stopping off at Bali for a couple of days on their way back

stop over *vi* (*stay briefly, especially referring to plane or passengers*) we stopped over at Manchester on the flight to Toronto

straighten out **1** *vtsep* **(a)** (*make straight*) he straightened out the crumpled bedclothes; **(b)** (*put right*) we need to straighten a few things out in this relationship; **2** *vi* (*become straight, referring to road etc*) after twisting and turning for a couple of hundred yards, the path finally straightened out

straighten up **1** *vtsep* **(a)** (*make straight*) he cannot pass a picture on the wall without straightening it up; **(b)** (*tidy*) straighten your room up a bit – it's very untidy; **2** *vi* (*rise from bending*) she straightened up and rubbed her back

strike back *vi* (*retaliate*) the government struck back at its critics with a strong defence of its actions

strike off *vtsep** (*delete from*) your name has been struck off

strike out **1** *vtsep* (*delete*) strike out whichever does not apply; **2** *vi* **(a)** (*hit out*) he struck out at his opponent; **(b)** (*go in stated direction*) we're all tired – let's strike out for home; **(c)** (*become independent*) I'm striking out on my own

strike up **1** *vt insep* (*begin*) the orchestra struck up a waltz; they struck up a friendship at school; **2** *vi* (*begin to play, referring to orchestra etc*) the band struck up

string along *vtsep Fam* (*deceitfully encourage someone*) that garage is just stringing you along – the car can't possibly be repaired; he just strung her along till he'd taken all her money and then he vanished

string up *vtsep Fam* (*hang*) they should string child abusers up from the nearest lamp post

strip down *vtsep* (*take apart, especially referring to machine*) the garage can't find the fault without stripping the engine down

strip off **1** *vtsep** (*remove*) the wind stripped all the leaves off the trees; he stripped off all his clothes and jumped into the water; we'll have to strip off about six layers of paint from this door; **2** *vi* (*remove clothes*) strip off and let the doctor examine you

sum up **1** *vtsep* **(a)** (*summarize*) the chairman summed up the committee's discussions; **(b)** (*assess quickly*) summing up the situation, he . . .; **2** *vi* (*summarize*) when summing up, the judge warned the jury against . . .

summon up *vtsep* (*collect one's strength etc with an effort*) I summoned up all my courage and asked to speak to the manager

swallow up *vtsep* (*engulf*) I watched them walk down the road and they were soon swallowed up by the mist; the sea swallowed them up

swear in *vtsep* (*give oath to*) when the witness had been sworn in . . .; the new president was sworn in today

sweat out *vtsep* **(a)** (*get rid of by sweating, referring to illness etc*) have a sauna and sweat your cold out; **(b)** (*endure*) you were found guilty and now you're just going to have to sweat it out

switch back *vi* (*revert to*) we tried electricity but we've decided to switch back to gas

switch off/on **1** *vtsep* (*turn electrical appliance off/on*) switch the radio off/on; **2** *vi* where does the power switch off/on?

switch over *vi* (*change channels on television*) will I switch over? – the news is on the other side

switch round *vtsep* (*exchange one for the other*) someone's switched these photographs round – they're not in the right frames

T

tail away/off *vi* (*diminish*) the noise of the lorry tailed away in the distance; her voice tailed off as she realized that no one was listening

tail back *vi* (*accumulate, of vehicles*) the traffic tailed back all the way to the intersection

take aback *vtas* (*astonish*) he quite took me aback with his insolence; the enemy was completely taken aback by the speed of our attack

take after *vipo* (*resemble, usually referring to children and parents*) don't blame me – it's her father she takes after

take apart *vtsep* **(a)** (*dismantle*) the radio hasn't worked since he took it apart; **(b)** *Fam* (*in sport, defeat severely*) who would have expected the Wimbledon title-holder to be taken apart by a completely unknown player?

take around *vtsep** (*show around*) would you like someone to take you around?

take away **1** *vi* (*diminish*) having to go home by public transport takes away from the pleasure of going out; **2** *vtsep* **(a)** (*subtract*) what do you get if you take 28 away from 70?; **(b)** (*remove*) they took the man next door away in an ambulance last night; **(c)** (*buy prepared food*) how about some curry to take away?

take back **1** *vtsep* **(a)** (*return to place of origin*) take these library books back, will you?; **(b)** (*reclaim*) when is Tony coming to take back those records you borrowed?; **(c)** (*retract*) now that I know her better, I take back all that I said about her; **(d)** (*accept return of*) will the shop take it back if it doesn't fit?; she's a fool to take him back; **2** *vtas* (*remind*) these old songs take me back to when I was a teenager

take down *vtsep* **(a)** (*remove from high place, wall etc*) it's time we took the curtains down for a wash; take all your posters down; **(b)** (*dismantle*) when are the workmen going to take down the scaffolding?; the shops still haven't taken down their Christmas decorations; **(c)** (*note in writing*) the reporter took down very little of what was said at the meeting

take home *vtsep* (*earn*) how much does she take home every week?

take in *vtsep* **(a)** (*carry to a place*) take your coat in to the cleaner's tomorrow; **(b)** (*shelter*) they take in all the stray cats in the neighbourhood; taking in lodgers is not my idea of fun; **(c)** (*tighten*) could you take this skirt in?; **(d)** (*absorb*) he reeled off so many facts and figures that I couldn't take them all in; **(e)** (*include*) the Prime Minister's tour will take in a number of urban renewal projects; **(f)** Am (*go to see*) do you want to take in a movie?; let's take a few of the sights in first; **(g)** (*deceive*) he took the old lady in by telling her he had known her son; don't be taken in by appearances

take off **1** *vi* **(a)** (*leave the ground, referring to aircraft*) we took off an hour late; **(b)** *Fam* (*begin to improve*) the company's sales really took off last month; **(c)** *Fam* (*leave*) they're taking off for France next week; he's taking off early tonight (*ie from work*); **2** *vtsep* **(a)** (**remove*) take your hat off; the policeman was taken off the murder enquiry because he knew the people involved; **(b)** (*amputate*) they had to take her leg off below the knee; **(c)** (*reduce weight, price*) he needs to take a few pounds off; the saleswoman took a pound off the dress because of this stain; **(c)** (*make holiday of*) why don't you take the rest of the day off?; **(d)** (*imitate*) he takes the president off extremely well

take on **1** *vi Fam* (*be distressed*) don't take on so, he's not badly hurt; **2** *vtsep* **(a)** (*be responsible for*) when I married you I didn't realize I'd be taking on your whole family too; she's exhausted with all the extra work she's been taking on recently; **(b)** (*recruit*) that new electronics firm took on 200 people this week; **(c)** (*compete or fight with*) it was a mistake to take on the best snooker player in the club; why did you agree to take him on? – he's twice your size; **(d)** (*assume*) his face took on a cunning look; life has taken on a whole new meaning since I met you; **(e)** (*take aboard*) the train made an unscheduled stop to take on passengers

take out *vtsep* **(a)** (*remove*) if you want to work in the garage, you'll have to take the car out; washing won't take that stain out – the dress will have to be dry cleaned; **(b)** (*extract*) I'm having two teeth taken out tomorrow; **(c)** (*withdraw, especially money*) how much do you think we need to take out of our account?; **(d)** (*escort someone as a social activity*) he took her out to dinner at a very fancy restaurant; **(e)** (*obtain*) have you taken out insurance on the new car?; how about taking out a subscription to this computer magazine?; **(f)** (*vent one's negative feelings*) why should he take his anger out on us?; **(g)** (*set phrase*) (*tire*) kids take a lot out of you; that really took it out of me; **(h)** *Fam* (*destroy*) our men took out three enemy encampments

take over **1** *vi* (*assume control*) the new chairman will take over next week; we ought to do something about the garden – the weeds are taking over; **2** *vtsep* **(a)** (*assume control of*) she will be taking over the running of the hotel; **(b)** (**show round*) a guide will take you over (*the house*)

take round *vtsep* **(a)** (*carry to a place*) take this cake round to your grandmother's for me; **(b)** (**show round*) the supervisor was asked to take the trade delegates round (*the factory*)

take to *vipo* **(a)** (*develop liking for*) I've never really taken to the people next door; **(b)** (*develop habit of*) he has taken to treating me like an enemy; **(c)** (*escape*) the outlaws took to the hills

take up 1 *vi* (*continue*) to take up where I left off . . .; **2** *vtsep* **(a)** (*lift*) during their search, the policemen even took up the floorboards; she took up the newspaper and pretended to read; **(b)** (*carry upstairs*) take this tray up to your mother; **(c)** (*shorten*) these curtains need to be taken up a couple of inches; **(d)** (*occupy*) I've taken up too much of your time; the bed is so large it just about takes up the entire room; **(e)** (*discuss*) I think you should take the question of training up with the personnel manager; **(f)** (*start hobby, job etc*) he must be mad taking up jogging at his age!; when she first took up the appointment . . .; **(g)** (*accept*) I'm going to take up that offer of a weekend in the country; **(h)** (*continue*) her sister took up the thread of the conversation

take up on *vtaspo* (*argue with*) the Leader of the Opposition took the Prime Minister up on that last point

take upon *vtaspo* (*accept responsibility for*) you took that task upon yourself; why did she take it upon herself to call the police?

take up with *vipo* (*become friendly with, especially socially unacceptable people*) I'm afraid he has taken up with a bad lot

talk at *vipo* (*address, especially in pompous fashion*) he tends to talk at people rather than to them

talk away **1** *vi* (*continue to talk*) the old lady was talking away about her youth; **2** *vtsep* (*spend time talking*) we talked half the night away

talk back *vi* (*be impertinent, especially of children*) don't talk back to your father!

talk down **1** *vi* (*be condescending when speaking*) I wish she wouldn't talk down to me – I'm not stupid; **2** *vtsep* (*guide aircraft to ground by verbal instructions*) the fog was so thick at the airport that several planes had to be talked down

talk over *vtsep* (*discuss*) they've decided to talk things over and see if they can reach some kind of agreement

talk round **1** *vtas* (*persuade by talking*) Dad won't let me go to that pop concert – could you try talking him round?; **2** *vipo* (*not discuss directly*) they seemed nervous about tackling the problem head on and just talked round it

tamper with *vipo* (*interfere with, touch, especially with criminal intent*) after the car accident, he claimed that the brakes had been tampered with

tangle up *vtsep* **(a)** (*make confused*) the kitten tangled all the wool up; **(b)** (*catch*) he got tangled up in the barbed wire when he tried to climb the fence; **(c)** (*involve*) I'm sure she's tangled up in something dishonest

tangle with *vipo Fam* (*quarrel or fight with*) he tangled with a drunk about some stupid football game

tear apart *vtsep* **(a)** (*destroy*) the country is being torn apart by civil war; **(b)** (*search thoroughly and untidily*) the police tore the place apart looking for drugs

tear away **1** *vtsep* (*remove by tearing, especially covering of some kind*) I tore away the wrapping paper; **2** *vtas* (*leave reluctantly*) if you can tear yourself away from that television set for a minute . . .

tear into *vipo* (*attack physically or verbally*) the lion tore into the flesh of the deer it had killed; the boss tore into me for being late for the meeting

tear off *vtsep** (*detach by tearing*) she tore the label off the suitcase

tear up *vtsep* **(a)** (*tear into small pieces*) his letter made her so angry she tore it up and threw it in the fire; **(b)** *Fig* (*cancel*) the football player threatened to tear up his contract if the club didn't pay him more

tell off *vtas* (*scold verbally*) I told him off for his impudence

tell on *vipo* (**a**) (*affect badly*) the strain of waiting for news is telling on her; (**b**) (*inform on*) Mum knows about the practical joke we were planning – someone must have told on us

thaw out *vi* (*defrost*) leave the meat to thaw out; *Fig* have a cup of tea and thaw out

thin out **1** *vi* (*become less dense*) he's thinning out on top (*ie his hair is*); audiences are thinning out; **2** *vtsep* (*make less dense*) thin the plants out in autumn

think about *vipo* (**a**) (*reflect on*) it's strange that you should have phoned just when I was thinking about you; (**b**) (*consider doing without having reached firm decision*) I'm thinking about going to the cinema tonight – do you want to come?

think back *vi* (*reflect on past events*) the policemen asked him to think back and try to remember what had happened; thinking back, I don't believe we did send them a Christmas card

think of *vipo* (**a**) (*be attentive to*) it's about time she started thinking of herself instead of other people all the time; (**b**) (*recall*) I can't think of his telephone number at the moment; (**c**) (*imagine*) just think of it – a holiday in the Caribbean!; (**d**) (*have opinion about*) what do you think of the latest fashions?; I don't think much of their new house; (**e**) (*consider*) we wouldn't think of letting our daughter hitchhike across Europe on her own; (**f**) (*have idea*) who thought of coming to this restaurant?; I've thought of a solution to the problem

think out/through *vtsep* (*consider thoroughly*) have you thought out the effect that this proposal will have on our employees?; let's think things through

think over *vtsep* (*consider before making a decision*) I told him I would think his offer over

think up *vtsep* (*devise*) they've thought up a brilliant idea

throw away *vtsep* **(a)** (*discard*) throw those old papers away; **(b)** (*foolishly waste opportunity, money etc*) she threw away her chance of a place at university; you're just throwing your money away buying all those records

throw back *vtsep* **(a)** (*return by throwing*) the fish was so small that the angler threw it back; **(b)** (*throw in backward direction*) she threw her head back

throw in *vtsep* (*provide in addition to what has been purchased*) the man in the furniture shop said that if we took the bed, he would throw in the mattress for thirty pounds

throw off *vtsep* **(a)** (*discard hastily*) he threw off his outer clothes and jumped into the river; **(b)** (*get rid of cold etc*) I can't seem to throw off this virus

throw out *vtsep* **(a)** (*discard*) don't throw those photographs out; **(b)** (*reject*) after discussion, the committee threw the proposal out; **(c)** (*eject*) the manager of the cinema threatened to throw the boys out if they didn't behave themselves

throw together *vtsep* **(a)** *Fam* (*make hastily*) it's not very well made, it looks a bit thrown together; **(b)** (*put together hastily*) he threw some clothes together in a suitcase and raced to the airport; **(c)** (*of people, bring into close contact*) friends threw the two of them together; on such a small cruise ship, everyone is thrown together, like it or not

throw up **1** *vi Fam* (*vomit*) no wonder you threw up, mixing your drinks like that; **2** *vtsep* (*abandon* *job, opportunity etc*) imagine throwing up a chance to go to the United States

tick off *vtsep* **(a)** (*mark with tick*) will you tick people's names off as they come in to vote?; **(b)** *Fam* (*reprimand*) the teacher ticked him off for being late

tick over *vi* (*function, of machine, business etc*) the restaurant is ticking over quite well

tide over *vtas* (*help for short period of time, especially with money*) could you lend me five pounds to tide me over until the end of the week?

tie down *vtsep* (*restrict*) children tie you down; I don't want to be tied down to any specific date

tie in *vi* (*correspond*) how does the suspect's story tie in with his wife's?

tie up **1** *vi* (*connect, make sense*) his debts, the robbery, and now a new car – it all ties up; **2** *vtsep* **(a)** (*make money impossible to spend*) his money is tied up until he is twenty-five; my capital is tied up in stocks and shares; **(b)** (*not be free, especially because of work*) she'll be tied up all this afternoon

tighten up *vtsep* **(a)** (*make tighter*) he bent to tighten up his shoelaces; **(b)** (*make more stringent*) they're tightening up the rules on tax shelters; the company has decided that security must be tightened up

tip off *vtsep Fam* (*warn or inform*) someone must have tipped him off that the police were on their way; the reporter was tipped off about an interesting story

tone down *vtsep* **(a)** (*make less bright etc*) we toned our original colour scheme down; **(b)** *Fig* (*moderate*) the reporter was told to tone his article down or the paper would be sued

top up *vtsep* (*give more to, especially of drink*) he kept topping my glass up; can I top you up?

touch down *vi* (*land, of aircraft, space capsule*) Concorde touched down exactly on schedule

touch up *vtsep* **(a)** (*apply small amounts of paint etc to improve appearance*) this bit of the window frame needs to be touched up; she's just gone to touch up her make-up; **(b)** (*touch sexually*) if you don't stop touching me up I'll slap your face

touch (up) on *vipo* (*make brief reference to*) his speech didn't even touch on the pollution problem

toughen up *vtsep* (*of person, make tougher*) he's one of those parents who send their sons to boarding school to toughen them up

trail away/off *vi* (*of voice, become silent*) his voice trailed away with embarrassment

trot out *vtsep Fam* (*produce or give, especially something used many times before*) don't trot out the same old excuses; he's not going to trot that speech out again, is he?

try for *vipo* (*attempt to obtain*) she is trying for a place at music school; he's trying for the record

try on *vtsep* (*put on clothes, shoes etc with a view to buying*) I've been trying dresses on all morning

try out *vtsep* (*test*) the football club is trying him out in goal; you can have the car for a day to try it out

turn against **1** *vipo* (*become opposed to*) why have you turned against me?; **2** *vtaspo* (*make opposed to*) she claims that her ex-husband is turning their children against her

turn back **1** *vi* (*return in same direction*) we turned back because the path had become too faint to follow; **2** *vtsep* **(a)** (*refuse entry*) the refugees were turned back at the border; **(b)** (*fold*) she reluctantly turned back the bedclothes and got up; **(c)** (*of watch etc, move hands back*) we turned our watches back an hour

turn down *vtsep* **(a)** (*smooth down*) since the rain had stopped, he turned his coat collar down; **(b)** (*reduce heat, sound etc*) turn the gas down a bit; please turn the radio down – it's far too loud; **(c)** (*not accept*) I've been turned down for that job I applied for; she turned down his offer of a weekend in Paris

turn in **1** *vi Fam* (*go to bed*) it's late – why don't we turn in?; **2** *vtsep* **(a)** (*betray to police*) his former wife turned him in; **(b)** (*give to authorities*) at the end of the war, lots of soldiers kept their handguns as souvenirs instead of turning them in; hundreds of weapons were turned in during the amnesty

turn off **1** *vi* (*leave road to take another*) you turn off at the second street on the left; **2** *vtsep* **(a)** (*stop radio, water, engine etc*) be sure to turn the stove off; who didn't turn the tap off?; **(b)** (*disgust*) people who pick their noses in public turn me off

turn on **1** *vtsep* **(a)** (*start, referring to machine, television etc*) turn the gas on for me; **(b)** (*please greatly, often sexually*) rock music turns her on; he is turned on by her; **2** *vipo* **(a)** (*attack physically or verbally, taking by surprise*) one of her dogs turned on her; he turned on me when I suggested that he retire; **(b)** (*depend on*) the company's success turns on the skills of its employees

turn out **1** *vi* **(a)** (*attend*) not many people turned out for his funeral; **(b)** (*transpire*) it's one of those silly stories where the heroine turns out to be a lost heiress; **(c)** (*be, in the end*) how did the cake turn out?; everything will turn out fine; **2** *vtsep* **(a)** (*switch off*) it's time you turned the light out and went to sleep; **(b)** (*empty*) I turned out my handbag to look for my keys; **(c)** (*produce*) we're now turning out 100 computers a day; **(d)** (*eject*) the old man was turned out of his cottage

turn over **1** *vi* (*change position by turning*) he turned over in bed; the lifeboat turned over and sank in seconds; **2** *vtsep* **(a)** (*surrender*) the suspect was turned over to the police; they have turned the running of the restaurant over to their son-in-law; **(b)** *usually not separated* (*of business, make profit*) he must be turning over a good thousand a week

turn round **1** *vi* **(a)** (*face other way*) he turned round and looked at her; **(b)** *Fam* (*do something without warning*) he just turned round and punched the other chap; **2** *vipo* (*go round*) turn round the next corner; **3** *vtsep* **(a)** (*reverse bad situation*) the company was headed for bankruptcy but the new management team turned it round; **(b)** (*process, deal with*) how quickly can you turn this order round?; **(c)** (*move to face other way*) she turned the chair round and sat down

turn up **1** *vi* **(a)** *Fam* (*arrive*) he always turns up late; she turned up at the party with her new boyfriend; **(b)** (*be found*) if you're sure that you lost it indoors, then it's bound to turn up one day; **(c)** (*happen*) things always have a habit of turning up when you least expect them to; **2** *vtsep* **(a)** (*fold upwards*) he turned his collar up in the wind; **(b)** (*increase, make louder etc*) turn the television up will you, I can hardly hear; turn the heat up a bit

U

urge on *vtsep* (*encourage, with sense of urgency*) the marathon runner said he managed to finish the race only because the crowd urged him on; her family is urging her on to go to university

use up *vtsep* (*consume completely*) use up the last of the milk before it turns sour; the children used up all their energy playing

V

venture on *vipo* (*attempt, especially something foolish or risky*) he refused to venture on any criticism of the book until he had read it

verge on *vipo* (*be very close to*) I was verging on tears; the sailors were told that their behaviour verged on mutiny

vote down *vtsep* (*defeat by voting*) the amendment to the law was voted down

vote in *vtsep* (*appoint by voting*) the other members of the committee voted her in as chairwoman

vote on *vipo* (*decide by voting*) union members will be asked to vote on management's latest offer; it was voted on last night

W

wade in *vi Fam* (*take part in eagerly*) when the fight started, everybody waded in; our discussion wasn't really anything to do with her, but she waded in anyway

wade into *vipo Fam* (*attack with determination*) he got up early and waded into the job of cleaning the windows; I'm sorry – I shouldn't have waded into you for something so minor

wait behind *vi* (*stay*) she volunteered to wait behind until the doctor came

wait in *vi* (*wait at home*) I was late because I had to wait in for the telephone engineer

wait on **1** *vi* (*continue to wait*) he waited on in the hope that she would eventually arrive; **2** *vipo* (*serve*) the waitress who was waiting on them seemed to have vanished

wait up *vi* (*not go to bed*) don't wait up – I'll be very late

wake up **1** *vi* **(a)** (*waken*) she woke up when the church bells started ringing; **(b)** (*realize what is happening*) his mother never did wake up to the fact that he was a thief; **2** *vtsep* **(a)** (*awaken*) don't wake me up too early tomorrow; **(b)** (*make realize what is happening*) this country needs waking up

walk into *vipo* **(a)** (*enter*) she walked into the room; the suspect walked right into the trap the police had set for him; **(b)** (*collide with*) I almost walked into a lamp post

walk off **1** *vtsep* (*get rid of by walking*) let's go out and walk our Christmas dinner off; **2** *vi* (*leave*) he walked off and left us standing there

walk off with *vipo Fam* **(a)** (*win easily*) she walked off with all the first prizes for her flowers; **(b)** (*steal*) the bank manager has walked off with a million pounds; **(c)** (*take*) who keeps walking off with the scissors?

walk out *vi* **(a)** (*leave*) she walked out of the room; **(b)** (*leave abruptly*) you can't just walk out on your wife and children!

walk over *vipo* (*thoroughly defeat*) the champion walked all over another opponent today

walk through *vipo* (*succeed with little effort*) you'll walk through the job interview

walk up *vi* **(a)** (*go up on foot*) the lift was out of order so we had to walk up; **(b)** (*approach*) a complete stranger walked up and started talking to me

warm up **1** *vi* **(a)** (*become warmer*) I hope it starts warming up now that spring is here; **(b)** (*loosen* *muscles, referring to athletes etc*) tennis players get a couple of minutes to warm up before the match; **2** *vtsep* **(a)** (*heat*) warm up some soup for yourself; **(b)** (*make people ready for some kind of performance*) the star of the show doesn't appear until the other acts have warmed the audience up; **(c)** (*make more lively*) can't we do anything to warm this dinner party up?

warn off *vtsep** (*tell to stay away or not to do something*) I was going to buy it but someone warned me off

wash down *vtsep* (*swallow food, medicine etc with the help of liquid*) have a glass of wine to wash your meal down

wash off **1** *vi* (*disappear through washing*) do you think these stains will wash off?; **2** *vtsep** (*remove by washing*) just let me wash the oil off my hands

wash out *vtsep* **(a)** (*rinse*) wash your mouth out please; **(b)** *usually passive* (*be cancelled because of excessive rain*) the women's tennis final has been washed out

wash over *vipo* (*affect very little*) his mother's death seems to have washed over him; anything I say just washes over her

wash up **1** *vi* **(a)** *Br* (*clean dishes etc after meal*) whose turn is it to wash up?; **(b)** *Am* (*wash*) don't serve supper until I've washed up (*ie had a wash*); **2** *vtsep* **(a)** *Br* (*clean*) why I am always left with the greasy pots to wash up?; **(b)** *usually passive* (*to have no further chance of success*) he's washed up as a boxer; **(c)** (*of sea, carry to shore*) a body was found washed up on the beach

watch out *vi* **(a)** (*look carefully*) watch out for bones when you're eating the fish; **(b)** (*be careful*) watch out – you nearly broke the window

water down *vtsep* (*make drink, criticism etc less strong*) water this down with a drop of soda, will you?; the drama critic accused the editor of watering his review down

wave down *vtsep* (*stop vehicle by waving*) he didn't see the policeman waving him down

wave on *vtsep* (*instruct vehicle to continue by waving*) the border guard waved them on without looking at their passports

wear away *vtsep* (*erode*) the sea is wearing the coastline away

wear down *vtsep* **(a)** (*reduce through use*) I've worn the heels of my shoes down; **(b)** (*exhaust gradually*) she is worn down by looking after all those children

wear off *vi* (*disappear*) the effect of the anaesthetic is wearing off

wear out **1** *vtsep* **(a)** (*use up by wearing*) that's the second pair of shoes he's worn out in six months; **(b)** (*exhaust*) she's wearing herself out with the preparations for her daughter's wedding; **2** *vi* (*become old-looking through use*) the carpet is wearing out

weed out *vtsep Fig* (*remove by selecting*) we have weeded out the least promising candidates

weigh down *vtsep* (*impose burden on*) don't weigh me down with anything more to carry; *Fig* they are both weighed down with grief

weigh in *vi* **(a)** (*be weighed on scales, referring to boxer, jockey, luggage*) the champion weighed in at just under the limit; have you weighed in yet?; **(b)** (*take part in discussion*) I wish she wouldn't keep weighing in with comments that are totally irrelevant

weigh up *vtsep* (*judge, form opinion of*) he boasts that he can weigh people up with a single glance;

weighing up the situation, she . . . .

while away *vtsep* (*fill time, especially while waiting for something to happen*) how did you while away all those hours you had to spend in the airport lounge?

whip away *vtsep Fam* (*remove quickly*) the waiter whipped our plates away before we'd finished eating

whip out *Fam* **1** *vtsep* (*take quickly from bag, pocket etc*) he whipped out his wallet; **2** *vi* (*go out quickly*) I'm just whipping out to the car for my briefcase

whip round *Fam vi* **(a)** (*go quickly*) whip round to the chemist's for me; **(b)** (*collect money*) we whipped round to get a retirement present for him

whip up *vtsep* **(a)** (*cause violent emotion in*) such speeches are intended to whip an audience up; **(b)** (*cause to appear*) what can we do to whip up support for the campaign?; **(c)** (*mix by beating*) whip up some cream; make an omelette by whipping up some eggs; **(d)** *Fam* (*prepare quickly, especially food*) I whipped up a meal for them

whisk away *vtsep* **(a)** (*remove with movement of hand*) whisk the wasps away from the jam; **(b)** *Fam* (*take away quickly*) the president was whisked away by helicopter

whittle away *vtsep* (*diminish gradually*) she is whittling away her opponent's lead; support for the government is being whittled away by its evident failure to control inflation

whittle down *vtsep* (*diminish, with implication of effort*) we've whittled the number of candidates down

win back *vtsep* (*regain*) he won back all the money he had lost the previous week

win out/through *vi* (*succeed despite opposition or after long time*) he finally won out over his parents' objections; we won through in the end

win over/round *vtsep* (*obtain support from, often by persuasion*) they are trying to win me over to the idea of a holiday abroad; she is charming and has quite won us over

wind down **1** *vtsep* (*gradually bring to end*) the company has decided to wind down its operations in that part of the world; **2** *vi* (*gradually come to an end*) we went home since the party was winding down

wind up **1** *vtsep* **(a)** (*start mechanism of watch etc*) the clock needs to be wound up; **(b)** (*bring to an end*) we wound up our holiday with a weekend in Paris; **(c)** *Fam* (*annoy, tease*) he really wound her up with those remarks about her dress; don't you know when you're being wound up?; **2** *vi* = end up

winkle out *vtsep Fam* (*obtain from, with some effort*) I finally winkled the information out of him; it's no good trying to winkle any money out of me

wipe off *vtsep** (*erase*) the teacher wiped the equation off the board; wipe that grin off your face!

wipe out *vtsep* **(a)** (*erase*) she has completely wiped out the memory of the crash; **(b)** (*exhaust money, energy*) his gambling debts wiped out his entire fortune; I feel wiped out (*ie exhausted*); **(c)** (*destroy, kill*) enemy fire wiped out the village; whole families have been wiped out by the disease

work in *vtsep* (*include in a report, speech etc*) I think we should work something in about the help we received from other people; work the other ingredients in

work off *vtsep* (*get rid of, referring to anger, excess energy* *etc*) she worked her anger off on the squash court

work on *vipo* **(a)** (*be involved in*) he is working on a new project; **(b)** (*use as basis*) we'll have to work on what we have; **(c)** (*persuade*) I've tried working on him but without much success

work out **1** *vi* **(a)** (*amount to*) how much do you make that work out to?; **(b)** (*succeed*) that relationship will never work out; **(c)** (*take exercise, especially in gymnasium*) she's been working out all morning; **2** *vtsep* **(a)** (*solve*) once you've worked out the problem . . .; they'll have to work things out between themselves – I'm not getting involved; **(b)** (*devise*) he's worked out a plan

work up *vtsep* **(a)** (*develop*) I can't work up any enthusiasm for this project; **(b)** (*excite*) she was getting all worked up at the prospect of a holiday

work up to *vipo* (*move towards*) he's working up to proposing marriage to her; it was easy to see what she was working up to

wriggle out of *vipo* (*avoid obligation, often by a trick*) why did you let them wriggle out of doing their homework?; you can't wriggle out of this one

write away for *vipo* (*obtain by letter*) if you want to know more, write away for our free brochure

write in *vi* (*send letter*) a great many viewers have written in with their comments about last week's programme

write off **1** *vtsep* **(a)** (*cancel*) his debts have been written off; **(b)** (*regard as useless*) the critics wrote the play off; **(c)** (*damage so as to make unusable, referring to cars etc*) she wrote her father's car off; **2** *vi* (*obtain by letter*) I've written off for tickets

write out *vtsep* **(a)** (*write in full*) have you written out your essay?; **(b)** (*write*) just write me out a cheque; the shop assistant wrote out the receipt; **(c)** (*remove from script, referring to character in play etc*) her part has been written out

write up *vtsep* (*prepare*) he's writing up a report on his business trip

Z

zap up *vtsep Fam* (*make more exciting or appealing*) the prose style could do with a bit of zapping up; they've certainly zapped up the colour scheme

zero in on *vipo* (*reach or find accurately*) the missile zeroes in on its target from a range of . . .; they immediately zeroed in on the one weak point in the argument

zip up **1** *vtsep* (*close with zip*) she zipped her skirt up; zip me up, will you?; **2** *vi* (*close with zip*) the dress zips up at the back

INDEX

The codes in this index of verbs refer to the verb patterns as explained on pages 16-19. A code containing a P9 indicates that this is an irregular verb (see pages 22-26). Verbs in *-ate* and *-ize* are always P4 and have been omitted. For verbs prefixed with *de-*, *dis-*, *mis-*, *out-*, *over-*, *re-* and *un-* see the second element of the verb. (*Am*) indicates that the American spelling is as explained under P5.

Forthcoming titles

ENGLISH SPELLING

★ Nearly 30,000 alphabetical entries
★ Colour-coded to identify common spelling mistakes
★ Helpful hints for improving spelling
★ Words of similar sound and meaning simply explained

142mm × 96mm/abt 400pp/plastic cover
ISBN 0 245-54832-7

ENGLISH SYNONYMS

★ 8,000 key words alphabetically listed
★ Synonyms grouped according to meaning
★ Parts of speech specified for each key word
★ Clear distinction between literal and figurative meanings

142mm × 96mm/abt 400pp/plastic cover
ISBN 0 245-54831-9

ENGLISH USAGE

★ Over 4,000 alphabetical entries
★ Practical guidance on all aspects of usage
★ Clear examples to illustrate spelling and grammar rules
★ Coverage of foreign and scientific terms

142mm × 96mm/abt 400pp/plastic cover
ISBN 0 245-54830-0